THE MIND

THE MIND

Its Nature and Origin

Christiaan D. van der Velde, MD

Prometheus Books

59 John Glenn Drive
Amherst, New York 14228-2197

Published 2004 by Prometheus Books

Inquiries should be addressed to
Prometheus Books
59 John Glenn Drive
Amherst, New York 14228-2197
VOICE: 716-691-0133, ext. 207
FAX: 716-564-2711
WWW.PROMETHEUSBOOKS.COM

08 07 06 05 04   5 4 3 2 1

Library of Congress Cataloging-in-Publication Data

Velde, Christiaan D. van der.
    The mind : its nature and origin / Christiaan D. van der Velde.
        p. cm.
    Includes bibliographical references and index.
    ISBN 1-59102-190-1 (alk. paper)
    1. Cognition. 2. Mind and body. 3. Mental representation. I. Title.

BF311.V45 2004
128'.2—dc22

2004004498

Printed in Canada on acid-free paper

To
Patricia Murphy–van der Velde
Patrice
Christiaan Jr.
Murphy
Diederick
Anne-Marie

CONTENTS

ACKNOWLEDGMENTS

I would like to express my appreciation to the following professionals for their analysis of the earlier drafts and their meaningful suggestions: Lawrence Carver, MD; Tom Dziadoz, PhD; Estelle Friedman, PhD; Wallid Jaziri, MD; Jonathan Pincus, MD; Luigi Saracino, MD; Hyam Shafner, MD; and Howard Tennen, PhD. Michael Balcerzak provided the illustrations. I am especially grateful for the valuable support of assistant editor Heather Ammermuller.

INTRODUCTION

Throughout his professional life, Sigmund Freud held the opinion that "no mind can exist without a brain." He made several attempts in 1895 to prove that cerebral processes precede psychological ones but failed, presumably because of the still-limited information of the anatomy and functions of the brain in his time.[1]

At this time of writing—one century after Freud's efforts and with the benefits of our comprehensive anatomical, physiological, and biochemical knowledge of the brain thanks to the dramatic advances in the neurosciences during the last three decades—we may raise the question: Have these advances made it possible to corroborate Freud's concept of a cerebral foundation of the mind? There are two answers: yes and no.

On the affirmative side, the occurrence of mental experiences evoked by electrical in vivo stimulation of the temporal cortex,[2] the metabolic acceleration in given brain regions preceding and during the performance of mental functions as demonstrated with brain imaging technology, and the loss of specific mental functions following lesions in given brain areas provide indisputable evidence of a fundamental role of the brain in mental events.

On the negative side, none of these findings has provided any indication that may suggest how cerebral events either cause or convert into mental states and mental functions. This absence not only suggests that Freud might not have fared better if today's sophisticated knowledge of the brain were available to him; it also perpetuates the long-standing dispute between the *materialists*, who, like Freud, view the mind as a product of the brain, and the *mentalists*, who conceive the mind to be a nonphysical yet autonomous entity.[3]

What may be the reason why, despite the unmistakable involvement of the brain in our mental activities, the numerous efforts undertaken over the last three decades to clarify the brain's role in mental events have continued to be in vain? I believe that a conceivable answer to this question lies in the fact that our mental experiences can only be *partially* explained as originating from brain activity. This becomes apparent when we analyze the common denominator of all mental experiences: *the phenomenon of cognition*. As elaborated in part 1, every mental activity, be it thinking, remembering, judging, anticipating, planning, or conceptualizing, involves two distinctively different components: (1) a *sense of knowing*, that is, a sense of having experienced previously, and (2) a *cognitive content*, that is, what it is that we know, think, remember, or plan.

These two components are fundamentally different in nature and origin. Each thought, memory, or idea has its "own" specific content, which is mentally reproducible and remains fairly constant during reproductions. This reproducibility and constancy of cognitive content indicate a lasting storage of cognitive content suggesting the involvement of specific cerebral processes. There now is ample evidence (presented in part 2) to suggest that the cognitive content of any mental experience or activity is determined by the *gestalt of internal images* and that these gestalts can be conceived as the results of specific brain functions.

In contrast, *there is no conceivable primary brain function to suggest a cerebral origin of our sense of knowing*. Yet it also is inconceivable that we could experience a sense of knowing without cognitive content and vice versa. Therefore, we may conclude that our sense of knowing is *inseparably associated with our experiencing cognitive content*.

This inseparable association suggests, in light of the absence of a cerebral origin of knowing, that our sense of cognition may evolve as a consequence of our experiencing cognitive content and thus is an *empirical, that is, purely experiential product.* According to this scenario, our capacity of cognition may be conceived as the result of an inextricable combination of (1) a *cerebral* process that is responsible for the actuation of internal images whose gestalts cause us to experience cognitive content and (2) an *empirical* process that somehow emanates from this cerebral experience and, in turn, imparts its content the quality of having experienced before. In other terms: *our sense of knowing may be conceived as an empirical epiphenomenon resulting from our experiencing cerebrally produced internal images.*

Is there such an empirical process that causes us to experience our internal images with a sense of knowing? Such a process does indeed exist. Throughout life we continually develop sets of two notions that reflect sets of two events that are opposites because one event is caused by a given quality whose absence causes the occurrence of its opposite, yet we *conceive* these events as interconnected because we cannot realize one event without realizing the other. For example, our notions of days and nights. For reasons explained in chapter 2, these inseparable notions have been denominated as *dialectical notions*, and their underlying events are referred to as *dialectical events.*

One such set of dialectical events is formed by our *visual percepts and our internal images,* which represent previously experienced visual percepts. Their dialectical interconnectedness, described in chapter 3, makes it possible to conceive how we empirically realize our internal images as reflections of previously perceived visual percepts and thus causes us to experience the gestalts (content) of our internal images with a sense of cognition. I should like to emphasize that this concept of dialectical notions is not a hypothetical idea created for our particular effort to understand the nature and origin of our mental experienced; it reflects the consequences of *naturally occurring events thus far overlooked for their dialectical relationship.*

Because cognition is the common denominator of all our mental experiences, the *cerebral-empirical* rationale of our capacity of cognition also offers a new approach to our understanding of the origin and nature of our mental experiences in general. The cerebral component of cognition* affords us to apply the latest discoveries in the neurosciences and so identify the cerebral correlates of our mental experiences; the empirical component makes it possible to conceive *how* these cerebral acitivies are experienced as mental events. The details of these experiences, and their explicatory potential for all psychological phenomena, mental functions, and the nature and origin of the mind, are the topics of this book, which is organized as follows.

Part 1 begins with a description of the differences between cognition and recognition and the likely age of the earliest manifestation of cognition in humans, followed by a discussion of the concept and formation of dialectical notions. The dialectical differences between internal images and actual visual percepts are then applied to illustrate how we experience internal images as the carriers of our sense of knowing and as the containers of cognitive content and thus serve as the fundamental cognitive units in all mental experiences and as the constituents of the mind. *Because visual percepts and internal images are, by virtue of their gestalts, our only experiences that provide us with cognitive content, they have a dominant place in all further discussions.*

The focus in part 2 is on the cerebral aspects of mental experiences. Fundamental to the discussions in this part is the differentiation of our sensory perceptions into two modalities: (1) perceptual experiences, which are *mentally reproducible* in and by themselves, which reflect explicit or declarative memory, and (2) sensory experiences, which are *not mentally reproducible* in and of themselves and reflect implicit memory. The processes by which the different forms of memories are stored, consolidated, and mentally or incidentally actuated are discussed by applying a recently introduced concept of *mnemonic fusions*. This concept emerged (see chap. 6) by utilizing the

---

*Cognitive neuroscientists distinguish between *explicit* (or declarative) and *implicit* (or intuitive) forms of cognition. The notion of cognitive *content* as a reflection of the gestalts of internal images as suggested above corresponds with explicit cognition and is the central subject of our discussions in part 1. The nature and origin of implicit cognition are discussed in part 2.

intricate network of neural connections between the various cerebral storage areas of the different categories of memory and explains the reciprocal interactions between explicit and implicit memory. The mnemonic fusions between the different forms of visual and auditory memory stored in the left and right hemispheres also enable us to explain the neurophysiological and psychological dynamics of language and conceptual thinking. The last chapter in this part describes how clinical and experimental findings suggest which cerebral regions may be involved in the actualization and coordination of mental experiences.

Part 3 summarizes why Freud's immortal concepts of the ego, the superego, the id, and the unconscious as permanent mental structures could not be explained by cerebral processes alone. The dual cerebral/empirical rationale of the mind makes it possible to conceive how we do indeed form *mental entities* that reflect the psychological properties of the traditional ego and superego but strictly are empirical products. The concepts of the id and the unconscious are conceived as natural, biological phenomena. This part concludes with a discussion of the phenomenon of dreaming. Its remarkable occurrences in four separate stages and its often bizarre contents provide support to the cerebral/empirical concept of psychological experiences.

Part 4 elaborates how the cerebral/empirical nature of psychological experiences may clarify the historical problems about brain, mind, and body interactions. The images we form of the bodily self and of the bodily appearances and behaviors of others are differentiated in *one's own body images* and *extraneous body images* of others. The combination of the dialectical nature of human encounters, and the mnemonic fusions formed between both categories of body images and with our emotional and somatic sensations experienced during previous interpersonal interactions, makes it possible to conceive a biopsychosocial rationale of body-mind and mind-body interactions, of the development of self-concept and personality, and of the psychodynamics of our social and interpersonal interactions.

Part 5 highlights the psychological and psychiatric implications of the cerebral/empirical theory in the development of personality, psychopathology, and psychotherapy.

NOTES

1. E. Jones, *The Life and Work of Sigmund Freud*, part 1 (New York: Basic Books, 1953).

2. W. Penfield et al., *The Mystery of the Mind* (Princeton, NJ: Princeton University Press, 1975).

3. P. S. Churchland, *Neurophilosophy: Toward a Unified Science of the Mind—Brain* (Cambridge, MA: MIT Press, 1986).

THE EMPIRICAL NATURE OF MENTAL EXPERIENCES

1

THE EMERGENCE OF COGNITION

Like all species, we humans start life in a mindless state. Once adults, we are incapable of undoing any of our mental functions and thus are unable to retrieve by introspective means how and when we developed our mental abilities. However, the remarkable studies and interpretations by Jean Piaget on cognitive development during infancy and childhood provide us with an opportunity to conceptualize the transition from the infant's initial state of naïveté to the first manifestation of cognition.[1]

Piaget believed that the first manifestation of cognition makes its appearance between the twelfth and eighteenth months of infancy (contemporary psychologists assume this to be several months earlier), when the infant's behaviors indicate the beginning of what Piaget designated as the *awareness of object permanence*. This concept refers to the infant's awareness of the existence of previously perceived objects even when they are temporarily out of sight. Piaget suggested that this awareness represents the most rudimentary form of the infant's use of memory and, thus, the beginning of cognition.

While this discovery played a monumental role in Piaget's conception of his now universally applied model of the sequential (sensorimotor-preoperational-operational-conceptual) stages of human intellectual development, it was of no avail in his career-long search for *psychological* mechanisms* to explain the transition from one developmental stage to the next, such as the emergence of the infant's awareness of object permanence during the sensorimotor stage. According to the views discussed in our introduction, Piaget's "failure" should not be surprising. Any approach to conceive the nature and origin of mental processes on a purely psychological foundation should be as futile as the failing efforts by the materialists to explain cognition on a purely biological basis. Another problem may have been the assumption that awareness of object permanence is humans' first manifestation of cognition, which I believe is not the case, as argued in chapter 3.

The infant's awareness of object permanence indicates that he has begun to experience internal images whose gestalts reflect previously perceived objects, as is evident from his looking for and later asking for an absent object. The question is: Does this awareness constitute the experience of "knowing" or "having experienced before"? If this is the case, we must note that some sense of "knowing" during infancy is already manifest long before the occurrence of object permanence by way of the phenomenon of *recognition.* Normally developing infants begin to show *within a few weeks postnatal* an ever-expanding ability to recognize the reappearances of the mother and her various actions associated with feeling and comfort. This indicates that the formation of *cerebral* representations of external objects and events begins during the earliest stages of human life and, when activated, are experienced as internal images,† which enable the infant to recognize recurring visual percepts of the reappearances of previously perceived objects.

It is most unlikely that the infant's and the very young child's experiences of recognition are of the same nature as we adults expe-

---

*While Piaget entered the field of epistemology as a biologist, he never mentioned a possible biological foundation for humans' cognitive development.[2]

†As discussed in chapter 12, the infant's earliest images of external objects are not experienced as partial reflections of objects as an entity but only as independent fragments of objects. It takes at least twelve months before the infant begins to perceive objects as perceptual entities.

rience them. As detailed at the end of this chapter, we adults experience three modes of cognition: *recognition, awareness of object permanence,* and *cognition,* that is, experiencing "independent" internal images (whose gestalts are not identical with the gestalts of simultaneously ongoing visual percepts) with a sense of having experienced before. The adult's sense of knowing has an epistemological quality, namely, we know *that* and *what* we know. The first manifestations of epistemological knowing are not apparent before approximately age five (see chap. 3). How, then, may we explain the infant's and the very young child's capacity of recognition or their awareness of object permanence without "knowing"?

This condition is not as paradoxical as it may appear. First, the capacity of recognition and awareness of object permanence are also apparent in *infrahuman species,* which are equipped with a visual sensory apparatus and a central nervous system that provides storage facilities for visual memory. These species do not appear to develop humans' sense of epistemological cognition, even though it may often seem that way.[3] Second, the adult's capacity of recognition is not the product of some mental function or mechanism but a *naturally, automatically, and irresistibly* occurring event, regardless of our epistemological sense of its occurrence. To illustrate how we may conceive the process that creates our experience of recognition, we analyze the following events, which most readers will have experienced in one variant or another.

A friend who just returned from his vacation in Switzerland visits us to show his snapshots. The first photo shows us the Matterhorn, the majestic mountain near the village of Zermatt in Switzerland, which we have never seen or heard of before. Our friend now places a second picture next to the first. *Looking at the two photos together,* we immediately "know": both photos reflect the same mountain but taken in slightly different angles. One month after this experience, we receive from our travel agent his promotional world calendar for the next year. While perusing the enticing pictures of the various vacation resorts in the world, we suddenly *recognize* the picture of the Matterhorn.

This example highlights the cardinal feature of our sense of having experienced before in recognition: *Its occurrence depends entirely upon the simultaneous experience of a recurring visual percept and the matching gestalt of an internal image.* This suggests that recognition is neither an innate function of the brain, nor a permanently acquired mental ability, but an empirical epiphenomenon, that is, the experiential consequence of the simultaneous occurrence of a recurring visual percept and its matching internal image.

While the notion of "having experienced before" in recognition is indistinguishable from that in our awareness of object permanence, there is a distinct difference between the two phenomena. During recognition, it is a *recurring visual percept* that we experience as having experienced before; during the awareness of object permanence, it is an *internal image* that we experience as having experienced before, *but in the absence of the original percept.* How, then, can we explain the infant's notion of having an internal image experienced before as suggested by his awareness of object permanence?

This is possible by applying a feature of our visual perception that is rather obvious yet still unacknowledged for its theoretical and practical significance: the *dual composition* of the gestalts that determine the content of visual percepts and internal images.

GLOBAL AND TRANSIENT GESTALTS

The gestalts of our visual percepts normally reflect two different contents: an overall view of the world around us, and within this global view we observe numerous objects that move in and out of our visual field. Therefore, we may conceive the content of our visual percepts to be composed of two different categories of gestalts: *global* and *transient gestalts.*

Global gestalts reflect the *structurally stationary* and *constantly visible* world around us: the sky; a landscape; a street with its rows of houses, billboards, and shops; and a laboratory with its walls, benches, and instruments. While global gestalts differ in "size" from a wide-angle view from an airplane to the narrow scope of the interior of an elevator, they *always involve the entire retina of both eyes* (detailed in chap. 7).

Transient gestalts are reflections of *mobile objects*, such as people, animals, and vehicles, which capriciously appear in and disappear from our global gestalts. Examples include clouds in the sky and the occupants of an elevator entering or leaving on different floors. Transient gestalts normally occupy only part of the retinas.

These differences between global and transient gestalts lead us to distinguish two functions of the global gestalts that are of paramount psychological significance. First, when we look down a busy shopping street, or are watching a sports event on television, our global gestalt remains constant for some time, yet its "inner" content continually changes because of the changing appearances and activities of transient objects. Consequently, *global gestalts provide the continuity of our visual perception and serve as "backdrop" against which we observe and later remember the alternating presence and absence of transient objects.*

Second, because no mobile object exists in isolation, transient gestalts are always perceived as part of some surrounding global gestalt. Therefore, global gestalts are *our mnemonic reference points or situational cues* without which we could not remember where we parked our car, where to look for a misplaced item, or where to meet someone for an appointment.

These two functions of global gestalts enable us to address the question of how we experience our internal images of transient objects with a sense of having experienced before, even when the object is out of sight, and despite the fact that the sense of having experienced before in recognition does not evolve as the product of a function of the brain or the mind but requires the simultaneous experience of internal images and visual percepts whose gestalts are identical.

When the infant experiences an internal image of the mother, he internally "sees" her transient gestalt as part of a global gestalt, which we assume, in view of the infant's restricted surroundings, to reflect the room in which he usually perceives the mother. If the mother is present during this internal experience, he will recognize the mother and the room, *but he will only be aware of the actual percept* due to the congruence of the gestalts of image and percept and the experiential dominance of the latter. If the mother is absent while he experiences her internal image, he will be aware of both global gestalts of image and percept because of their discrepant composition. (Only the global gestalt of the internal image contains the transient gestalt of the mother.) Because of the similarity between their global gestalts (the room), we assume (projecting our adult experiences) that the infant "sees" both image and percept and consequently experiences them with a sense of *reciprocal recognition* of the identical global gestalts of the room. Because the transient gestalt of the mother is an integral part of the internal global gestalt of the image, we assume that he also experiences the transient gestalt of the mother as having experienced before.

RECOGNITION AND OBJECT PERMANENCE VERSUS COGNITION

The "reciprocal recognition" rationale of the infant's awareness of object permanence as conceived above implies that this awareness is not the first manifestation of cognition, as Piaget suggested, because its occurrence is dependent upon recognition. This dependency is apparent from the awareness of object permanence in *infrahuman species*, as observed in the experiments by M. Mishkin and cowork-ers, as well as P. Goldman-Rakic and her team. They have shown with their career-long investigations of the neurophysiology of memory that monkeys, after a few trials, precisely "know" where to locate hidden peanuts in a laboratory testing field. This "knowledge" can be explained as an awareness of object permanence. It reflects the monkey's utilization of internal images. (Both Mishkin and Goldman-Rakic have shown that the *visual association cortex*, where we assume visual engrams to be stored, plays an essential role in the formation of the monkey's memory.) The location of peanuts in the gestalt of the internal images guides the monkey where to find peanuts when it visually perceives the global gestalt of the testing field matching the global gestalt of the internal image. The behaviors of monkeys do not suggest that, when they are moved away from the laboratory and spontaneously experience an internal gestalt con-taining peanuts, they begin to "think" where to locate the laboratory and the testing field. But when placed again in the familiar experimentation room, they immediately move to the testing area to "look for" peanuts. Thus, monkeys "know" only by reciprocal recognition by virtue of the simultaneous experience of a visual percept and internal image with matching global gestalts. (The role of olfactory and other sensory memories "attached" to internal images in the behavioral learning and adaptation of infrahuman species is discussed in chapter 6.)

These explanations are applicable to the one-year-old infant who seems to "know" where to locate a previously perceived toy now concealed under a pillow (one of Piaget's earliest experiments that led to his concept of the awareness of object permanence). He experiences an internal image whose global gestalt (the pillow) contains a transient gestalt (the toy), which guides him in "expecting and locating" the toy *when he perceives the "familiar" global gestalt of the pillow.*

However, there is a significant difference between the infant's awareness of object permanence and that of the adult. As elaborated later, the child's behaviors and developing verbalizations during the first four or five years indicate that the child does not clearly distinguish between internal images and actual visual percepts as we adults do. This distinction becomes apparent between the ages of four and six years in the form of abstract thinking (see chap. 3). Then it becomes apparent that the awareness of object permanence is not a transient phenomenon as part of early development but remains *throughout life* an independent and indispensable function, like recognition and cognition, highlighted in the following illustration of events with which most readers can identify.

We are driving home on a dark winter evening in miserable weather after a trying day in the laboratory. We received notice that a vital research grant application was approved but not funded; a power outage during the previous night had ruined a precious collection of frozen tissues and wasted months of arduous research. While pondering over the consequences of these disappointing events, the thought of a long vacation far away suddenly enters our mind. We now "see" the images of our friend's vacation snapshots of the Matterhorn, then remember our travel agent's calendar, which leads us to think of the excitement of traveling, passports, customs, foreign languages, and the enjoyment of beautiful sceneries. Again suddenly, our "dreams" come to an end when we find ourselves at home in our garage, getting out of the car. We then note with some amusement but without surprise that although our thoughts were so far "away" while driving, we still perceived and obeyed traffic lights, correctly negotiated turns to find our way home, and even spotted our neighbor's dog at some strange place.

This example indicates that we adults simultaneously exercise three modes of "knowing," all differing in chronological development, involving different mechanisms, and serving distinctly different "functions."

1. **Recognition.** Appears soon after birth. Experienced during the simultaneous occurrence of a recurring visual percept and its matching internal image as an *automatic and instantaneous happening* whenever we are engaged in visual perception (like obeying traffic lights or recognizing our neighbor's dog at some strange place).

2. **Awareness of object permanence.** Appears at the beginning of the second year of life. The combination of "reciprocal" recognition of a simultaneously occurring visual percept and internal image with identical global gestalts, with the latter also containing a transient gestalt. It enables us to "intuitively" find our way home (like negotiating correct turns) by virtue of the global gestalts of our internal images and corresponding visual percepts.

3. **Cognition.** A sense of knowing inextricably associated with the experience of internal images *whose gestalts are not congruous to the gestalts of ongoing visual percepts* (like dwelling on vacation plans). Despite the absence of "their" original visual percept, we experience these "independent" internal images with a sense of knowing *that* we know and *what it is that we know*, the hallmark of explicit cognition.

How and when have we come to realize internal images as such and visual percepts as such? How may we explain that we experience internal images with a sense of having experienced before in the absence of their original visual percepts? These issues can be addressed by applying the properties of two naturally occurring phenomena: *dialectical events* and *dialectical notions*.

NOTES

1. M. A. S. Pulasky, *Understanding Piaget* (New York: Harper & Row, 1980).

2. J. Nash, *Developmental Psychology* (Englewood Cliffs, NJ: Prentice-Hall, 1970).

3. R. D. Griffin, *The Questions on Animal Awareness* (Los Altos, CA: Kaufman, 1981).

2

DIALECTICAL EVENTS AND DIALECTICAL NOTIONS

The term *dialectic(al)* was introduced in 464 BCE by the philosopher Zeno of Elea to describe a particular mode of reasoning: arguing the validity of an idea or hypothesis by exposing the logical absurdity of its opposite. Plato declared Zeno's approach a supreme method of logic, and from then on, "dialectics" has been an important strategy in the solution of philosophical issues.

While the term has never lost its original connotations of *oppositeness* and *interconnectedness* during the two thousand years of its usage, its definitions and applications have changed with every philosopher who employed the dialectical approach for one purpose or another. The definitions and applications are so divergent that the literature on the subject has come to distinguish several classes of dialectical theories: Aristotle's (probability versus inconsistency), Socrates' (truth versus untruth), Immanuel Kant's (illusion versus enlightenment), G. W. F. Hegel's (synthesis via thesis and antithesis of opposites), and Karl Marx's (dialectical materialism), to name only the familiar ones. This bewildering diversity and the vagueness of definitions have led critics to label dialectics as "unintelligible nonsense."[1]

However, during every waking moment of our life, we constantly experience all sorts of events that are each other opposites in a given quality, yet they lead to sets of inseparably interconnected notions that can be most appropriately qualified as dialectical. Our notions of day and night are a typical example. These two notions are opposites because days reflect the quality of light whose absence "causes" darkness, which is the basis of our notion of nights. Even though we *experience* days and nights as independently occurring opposites, we *conceive* them as inseparably interconnected because we would not have realized the notion of days without realizing our notion of nights.

Thus, in contrast with Zeno's original use of dialectics to establish the truth of an idea by *eliminating* the veracity of its opposite, the term *dialectical* is here employed to refer to a set of two notions that reflect opposite qualities yet are *inseparably interconnected because we would not have formed either notion without forming the other*. Moreover, dialectical notions need not be "invented" by selecting opposing ideas as part of some reasoning process; we develop dialectical notions as a consequence of our experiences of *naturally occurring dialectical events* like days and nights, high and low tides. Dialectical events may be defined as sets of two events that are opposites because one event is caused by a *given quality* whose absence "causes" the occurrence of its opposite, yet the two events are conceived as interconnected because we realize the quality of one only by realizing the absence of that quality in the other.

What is the general usefulness of the concept of dialectics as conceived above, and how does it relate to our efforts to conceptualize the nature and origin of our sense of knowing? This concept makes it possible to clarify notions or concepts whose nature and origin cannot be understood in and by themselves but only by means of their dialectical counterparts if they are part of a set dialectical events. We develop our notion of light only by virtue of our experiences of darkness, our notion of gravity by means of weightlessness, and so do we develop our concepts of memory and perception thanks to our experiencing their underlying dialectical events as reasoned below.

FORMING DIALECTICAL NOTIONS

To form a set of dialectical notions is to realize their interconnectedness in spite of the independent occurrences of the opposite qualities of their underlying dialectical events. This realization involves the following three features that are characteristic of all our dialectical experiences.

First, dialectically related events continually *alternate* in appearance, as for example, the alternation between day and night, or high and low tide.

Second, the opposing qualities of dialectical events are reflected by physical objects. This makes it possible to perceive the alternating manifestations of dialectical opposites by means of physical objects, which, for the convenience of discussion, are referred to as *dialectical reflectors*. For example, the differences between day and night are reflected by our house; tidal changes are reflected by rising and declining water levels at the shore.

Third, during the waking states, we continually experience internal images while simultaneously experiencing visual percepts (see chap. 3). This makes it possible to *perceive* a given object (as dialectical reflector) reflecting the manifestation of the quality of one dialectical event while *simultaneously remembering* (by means of internal images) when the object reflected the absence of that quality. For example, we realize the interconnectedness between our notions of motion versus immobility by perceiving our parked automobile and simultaneously remembering how it moves over the road.

However, our ability to distinguish between *perceiving* and *remembering* as applied above reflects the utilization of functions of our still-unexplained capacity of cognition, *which we propose to clarify as the results of our experiencing internal images as dialectical events*. This seemingly premature use of our capacity of cognition is, in actuality, a classic example of *circulus in probando*, that is, solving a problem (such as the realization of the interconnectedness between two dialectically related events) with a premise (our capacity of cognition), which is to be explained by solving the primary problem. This circular intricacy reflects the fact that internal images and actual visual percepts not only are indispensable for the formation of all dialectical notions because their gestalts provide the perceptual and mnemonic reflections of all our visual experiences, *but they themselves constitute a set of naturally occurring dialectical events.* It is their dialectical relationship, elaborated below, that makes it possible to conceptualize the foundation of our capacity of cognition.

NOTE

1. R. Harre and R. Lamb, *The Encyclopedic Dictionary of Psychology* (Cambridge, MA: MIT Press, 1983).

3

COGNITION AS A DIALECTICAL EXPERIENCE

Internal images and visual percepts are dialectical events because we experience the gestalts of visual percepts with several qualities whose absence causes us to experience the same gestalts as opposites generally known as internal images. Visual percepts are experienced with a *sense of acuteness and crispness and as originating "out there"*; internal images lack the quality of actuality; their gestalts are vague and experienced as originating "within" (one's head or mind). The content (gestalts) of visual percepts *continually and unpredictably change* on account of the capricious appearances and disappearances of transient objects in our global visual field; internal images are reproducible at our discretion and their gestalts remain, *by and large*, constant as evident in any given memory. Furthermore, the *notions* we form of internal images and visual percepts are inseparably interconnected because we cannot realize visual percepts as such and vice versa.

While the dialectical interconnectedness of our notions of internal images and visual percepts as postulated above is axiomatic, the question arises: By which process or processes have we become aware of this inextricable relationship? It is generally taken for granted that our capacity to form notions in general is a function of our yet-to-be-clarified cognitive abilities. Contrary to this view, this chapter presents an attempt to illustrate that our experiences of the dialectical qualities of our internal images and visual percepts enable us to conceive how we come to realize our internal images as reflections of previously experienced visual percepts and that this *experiential realization constitutes the foundation of all our cognitive abilities.*

Our first step in this effort is to address a crucial yet easily overlooked detail. The intention to conceive how we come to realize internal images as such and visual percepts as such by means of realizing their dialectical interconnectedness implies that we must have established an awareness that internal images and visual percepts are different experiences. That these experiences are distinctively different is, to us adults, apodictic. However, children's play and verbalizations indicate[1] that they, until approximately age four, do not clearly distinguish between their internal images and visual percepts as is evident from the absence of a clear distinction between remembering (or fantasy) and perceiving (or reality). In contrast, we adults not only precisely know whether we are remembering or reperceiving a past event; we also experience our *independent* internal images with an *epistemological* quality, namely, *knowing that and what we know.**

The first manifestation of the child's differentiation between visual percepts and internal images becomes apparent between the ages of four and five. Piaget demonstrated this development by alternately pouring the same volume of water from one glass container into another container with twice the width of the first. The child under four maintains that the narrower container with the higher water level contains more water; the five- to six-year-old insists that the volumes are the same in both containers despite the different water levels. In another experiment, Piaget rolled a ball of clay into the shape of a sausage. The four-year-old considers the sausage an *irreversible* fait accompli and its weight and volume larger than those of the ball; the five- to six-year-old *knows* that the shape of the ball and the sausage are interchangeable and that their weights and volumes are equal.

---

*Although the *noun* epistemology is generally used to refer to the study of cognition, it is derived from the Greek term *epistanai*, which means *to understand*. Hence the use of the adjective epistemological as a reference to our "knowing that and what we know."

S. J. Bruner, J. H. Flavell, H. G. Furth, J. Nash, and M. A. S. Pulaski extended Piaget's experimentations and confirmed his findings and interpretations that permit us to draw three conclusions that pave the way for our current efforts to conceive the origin and nature of humans' capacity of cognition.[2]

The five-year-old child's verbalizations recorded during Piaget's studies and those of others indicate that the child has begun to experience internal images with a sense of knowing *that* and *what* she or he knows. This reflects (1) the child's first veritable experience of *epistemological cognition*, (2) that he or she experiences internal images and visual percepts as different events, and (3) that the child now has the ability to independently focus upon a selected internal image and thus is capable of engaging in *abstract thinking*.

How did these developments come about? Why does it take four to five years to occur? Piaget surmised that these developments are the consequences of the child's capacity of *reversibility*, that is, to realize that the sausage can be reversed into the ball of clay. This ability is considered among epistemological psychologists to be a cognitive operation. However, this exercise of reversibility is not (as is the case with the developing awareness of object permanence by the one-year-old infant) contingent upon the sense of cognition. The essential requirement for the child's awareness of the relationship between sausage and ball is the acquisition of internal images whose gestalts reflect the perceived change from ball to sausage. Until the age of four, the child's visual perceptions are focused on objects per se,[3] and the content of the corresponding internal images is restricted to that. The child then gradually expands his or her focus of perception and subsequently includes circumstances and details such as the molding of the ball into a sausage and the difference in water levels following the pouring of a given volume of water from one container into another.

These additional details are not added to the existing gestalts of earlier-formed internal images but are contained in the gestalts of newly formed imprints of each subsequent perception (see part 2). The accumulation of detailed gestalts eventually enables the child to compare the gestalts of internal images (reflecting the changes from ball to sausage or in water levels) with the visual perception of the gestalt of the end result. This suggests that "reversibility" is in principle a pictorial, thus neurophysiological, experience that does not require the function of cognition. In fact, it underscores the functional significance of the gestalts of internal images: they determine the content of knowledge.

The simultaneous emergence of cognition and differentiation as manifested by abstract thinking may suggest that the latter is the result of the former. However, according to the postulates advanced in the previous sections, this is not possible, since we assume that our capacity of cognition is based on our realizing internal images as reflections of previously experienced visual percepts, and such realization cannot occur without having differentiated between them. On the other hand, this differentiation requires realizing internal images *as such* and visual percepts *as such*, and these realizations cannot be explained without having explained our capacity of cognition. This represents thus an explicatory interdependence that we classified on page 31 as a *circulus in probando*. It is the combination of this explicatory interdependence, and the indispensability of internal images and visual percepts as content providers and their dialectical interconnectedness summarized in the introduction of this chapter, that suggests the possibility that our capacity of cognition and our awareness of differentiation could be conceived as two *independent yet inextricably associated* empirical epiphenomena resulting from the child's experiences of the dialectically related internal images and visual percepts.

The only available strategy to pursue these considerations is to analyze, by means of our fully established cognitive abilities, how we adults experience the dialectical differences yet interconnectedness between our internal images and visual percepts and how these experiences correlate with our intellectual activities and so enable us to conceive the transition from naïveté to the epistemological beginnings during our preschool years.

DIFFERENTIATING BETWEEN INTERNAL IMAGES AND VISUAL PERCEPTS

When we sit down at the end of the day and reflect upon the day's events, our own activities, and encounters with others, we avail ourselves of our capacity to *volitionally* and *selectively* actualize internal images at any given time. (The underlying process and actual nature of such actualization is detailed in chapters 10 and 18.) This capacity not only causes us to become aware that we have a certain control over internal images that we do not have over our visual percepts, it also keeps us constantly aware that internal images are our permanent *possessions* that are stored somewhere in our mind or head, *constantly accessible* and whose *content* (gestalt) remains the same* during each actualization.

These qualities cannot be realized *as such* by just experiencing them. This is also true for our experiencing the absence of these qualities in visual percepts that we experience as originating extraneously, whose occurrences are beyond our control and whose gestalts constantly change in content. I postulate that it is by virtue of our *simultaneously experiencing* these opposite qualities that we realize the experiential qualities of internal images described above as such by commutually realizing the absence of these qualities in visual percepts. But by what means do we come to *identify* these empirical, that is, nonphysical, qualities "as such"?

As the inescapable effect of environmental *auditory sensory input* from early development on, we have come to verbally describe our diurnal experiences of light and darkness in terms of days and nights, rising and receding water levels as high and low tides. And so did we learn to verbally refer to experiencing our volitional control of our internal images as *I remember, I retrieve my* memories.† *These*

---

*Sameness refers only to the gestalt (content). It does not include sameness of associated memories of past emotional or somatoceptive experiences because any given gestalt can be mnemonically fused with a variety of them (see chap. 6).

†The process by which experiential qualities are linguistically memorized is discussed in chapter 9.

verbalizations are referrals to qualities that eventually lead to our collective notion of selfness, while the absence of these qualities in visual percepts causes us to conceive the latter as nonself events.

We presume, therefore, that when the four- to five-year-old child begins to actualize internal images, as is evident from his or her emerging capacity of abstract thinking, he or she also begins to experience the visible aspects of dullness and vagueness of internal images as inextricably associated with the qualities of selfness, while the crispness and vivaciousness of visual percepts are inseparably experienced with a sense of nonself. The consistency of the self and nonself qualities explains how the child begins to experience his or her internal images and visual percepts as distinctively different events regardless of the alternations of a given gestalt from image to visual percept that occur during his or her daily activities.

The notion that the simultaneous occurrences of internal images and visual percepts result in the experiences of selfness and nonself is supported by our adult experiences. While the notion of selfness of internal images is to every normally functioning adult as natural and self-evident as one's heartbeat and respiration, the *origin* of our selfness and of our eventual self-concept has been as enigmatic as our capacity of cognition. This problem also exists with the notion of the nonself quality of the external world and its objects around us as emphasized by Immanuel Kant in 1871, when he accused his fraternity of philosophers of "the scandal of philosophy's inability to prove that objects exist outside ourselves."[4] This accusation still stands unchallenged.

These enduring enigmas reflect, I believe, the fact that explicatory efforts in the past approached our notions of self and nonself as psychological entities *in and of themselves*, whereas these entities are dialectically *thus inextricably interconnected*. They are dialectical in origin because our sense of selfness of our internal images reflects qualities whose absence in visual percepts causes us to experience these percepts with the notion of nonself, yet neither notion can be realized as such without realizing the opposite notion. This exemplifies par excellence the explicatory potential of our concept of dialectics, that is, to elucidate a notion or phenomenon whose origin or nature is incomprehensible in and by itself—like our concept of self—but becomes intelligible if it can be identified as a component of a given set of naturally occurring dialectical events, like internal images and visual percepts.

Because *notions in general* are the products of our cognitive abilities, we need to emphasize that our notions of self and nonself are the *epistemological reflections* (explained momentarily) of empirical qualities experienced only by virtue of the simultaneous occurrences of the natural events we have come to call our internal images and visual percepts. *We are, and inescapably so, the experiential recipients of the dialectically opposed qualities of selfness and nonself.*

Having conceptualized how during the fourth or fifth year of development we become aware of internal images and visual percepts as distinctively different events, we are now in a position to approach the question of how we, during the preschool years, came to realize that internal images are reflections of previously experienced visual percepts that (i.e., the realization) we propose to be the foundation of our capacity of cognition and that ultimately enables us to form *our notions* of self and nonself.

REALIZING INTERNAL IMAGES AS REFLECTIONS OF PREVIOUSLY EXPERIENCED VISUAL PERCEPTS

Cognition is synonymous with remembering, knowing, or having experienced before; its dialectical counterpart is visual perception.

The suggestion that our notions of remembering and perceiving also are derivatives of the dialectical qualities of internal images and visual percepts prompts the question: How can one single set of events result in two different sets of dialectical notions?

First, our notions of selfness and nonself are reflections of specific *differences* between internal images and visual percepts, while our notions of remembering and perceiving reflect their *interconnectedness*.

Second, the experiences that underlie the two sets of notions are antipodal in *dialectical dominance*. Internal images are the dominant events in our notions of selfness versus nonself because we experience their gestalts with a sense of selfness that is absent in visual percepts, yet visual percepts are, as acute, bright, and sharp sensory experiences, dominant over internal images because the latter are experienced as inert, dull, and vague reflections of visual percepts.

Third, the formation of the two sets of notions involves different processes. Our notions of selfness and nonself are purely *empirical* derivatives as just described, while our notions of remembering and visual perception are based on *visible thus material* opposites, namely, the brightness, sharpness, and vivaciousness of the gestalts of visual percepts as opposed to the dull and vague gestalts of internal images. We are involved in both processes because we serve not only as the *experiential recipients* of the empirical qualities of selfness versus nonself; we *concurrently* are the *internal observers* of the opposite visible features of the gestalts of internal images and visual percepts. (The contiguity of the empirical and visible experiences explains how the five-year-old child begins to experience internal images and visual percepts as inextricably associated with the sense of selfness and nonself respectively and so differentiate internal images from visual percepts.)

Finally, realizing internal images as reflections of *previously* experienced visual percepts involves two fundamentally different experiences: (1) seeing internal images as reflections of visual percepts *by means of the visible aspects of their gestalts* and (2) the accompanying sense of having experienced before, *which represents another empirical epiphenomenon.*

EXPERIENCING INTERNAL IMAGES AS REFLECTIONS OF VISUAL PERCEPTS

From the very moment we awaken through the last seconds before drifting into our nocturnal slumber, we are *continuously* subject to visual sensory input, while the cerebral areas that contain the neuronal substrates of our stored internal images are *incessantly activated* by cerebral sources (see chap. 10). Consequently, we are during the waking states constantly and irresistibly engaged in the simultaneous and continuous experiences of the three cognitive modes identified in chapter 1: *recognition* (of our ceaseless perceptions of our familiar environment), *awareness of object permanence* (awareness of the existence of temporarily absent transient objects or events in a familiar milieu), and *abstract cognitive experiences* by means of independent internal images whose gestalts are not congruent with the gestalts of ongoing visual percepts.

The first two modes provide us with uninterrupted opportunities to experience the three dialectical factors that enable us to realize the *interconnectedness* between internal images and visual percepts, that is, realizing the former as reflections of the latter and the latter as the origin of the former. Whether we move in our house from room to room while preparing for our daily chores, drive from one street to the next while en route to the office, or roam through the aisles of a library in search of some publication, all our movements are initiated and guided by the global and transient content of the gestalts of our internally activated internal images. The moment we arrive in a room, or at a street or library section as planned, the gestalt of the guiding internal image is now experienced as an actual visual percept and thus creates the sense of recognition, confirming that we implemented our intentions. Later on, when reviewing our earlier activities during the day by screening the internal images we formed of our visual percepts during the day's actions, we know that these images reflect actually experienced visual percepts, thanks to the continuous occurrences of visual percepts even though their gestalts are unrelated.

These recursive alternations of *given gestalts* from image to visual percept and *vice versa* thus comply with two of the three factors required for our realizing the interconnectedness between dialectical notions in general: the *alternating* occurrences of visual dialectical qualities (sharpness versus darkness) and *dialectical reflectors* in the form of a given gestalt. The third factor (our ability to simultaneously *perceive* the brightness of gestalts and *remember* our experiencing them as dark) is the very object of our explanatory efforts, namely, our sense of having experienced before, which requires a separate discussion.

THE NOTION OF HAVING EXPERIENCED BEFORE

To put the essentials of this task in clear perspective, I utilize a domestic event that most readers will have experienced in one way or another. It is early in the morning, and we are about to leave for our office when we remember to retrieve our briefcase containing reports that we studied the previous night in preparation for today's activities. Accordingly, we walk to our den and look at the chair next to our desk, but there is no briefcase. We now try to remember where else we might have placed the briefcase by screening the global gestalts of our internal images that reflect our visual observations of our activities and whereabouts during the previous night. After a few minutes of this internal perusal, it suddenly occurs to us that we, just before retiring, had decided to place the briefcase in our car to be certain that we would not forget it (!) the next morning.

What caused this lapse of memory? How were we, during this transient amnesia, capable of retrieving and actualizing the pertinent internal images? How are we aware of the existence of stored internal images of previous events and actions without remembering them? How do we experience the eventually activated internal images with that distinctive notion of *having experienced their original visual percepts the night before*?

Having experienced before is a paradoxical phrase. It reflects a truism because all normally functioning humans experience their internal images with a sense of having experienced before, yet it seems absurd that one can have an awareness of a previous visual experience without reexperiencing it. However, it appears possible to clarify this absurdity by means of combining our experiencing internal images as passive reflections of visual percepts as just described with another empirical feature unique to internal images. We experience them not only as permanently stored and constantly accessible mnemonic entities but also with *an awareness that all internal images are chronologically stored according to the sequential occurrence of their original visual percept* (when, for instance, we review our activities of yesterday or reminisce particular events while in college or during high school or childhood). Consequently, we experience our internal images as elements of a *temporally cohesive reservoir of latent images*, conveniently referred to as our *visual memory bank*.

In light of the empirical nature of our sense of having experienced before, the question arises: By which process or processes have we memorized the chronology of the occurrences of our past perceptual experiences? A possible answer to this question emerges by applying the combination of a second category of visual perceptions that lead to the formation of *linguistic engrams* and the earlier-mentioned concept of *mnemonic fusions*.

The term *mnemonic fusions* refers to the mnemonic interconnectedness between the memories of two different kinds of sensory experiences, established by virtue of the formation of neural connections between the specific cerebral areas where the engrams of the simultaneously experienced sensory modalities are stored (details in chap. 6). Mnemonic fusions are formed between any set of sensory experiences. They are formed automatically and irresistibly. Because their connecting neural pathways are bidirectional, the activation of one memory automatically and instantaneously actuates the memory of its counterpart.

The formation of neural interconnections between engrams of various sensorial experiences is evident in human infants as early as three weeks postnatal—years before the unfolding of cognitive awareness. *This indicates that they are not the products of mental activities*. During these early years of development, their formation is restricted to acoustic and visual engrams and the pain and pleasure centers in the limbic system and have a significant influence upon the child's interactions with the environment (see chap. 6).

The formation of linguistic engrams normally begins in the first grade as the result of the visual perceptions of *written or printed words and digits*. The interesting feature of these visual engrams is the fact that they are not formed in the same (i.e., right) cerebral hemisphere where our global visual engrams are formed. As discussed in chapter 9, linguistic visual engrams are in 90 percent of adults (even if they are left-handed) cast in the associative occipital cortex of the *left hemisphere*.

Linguistic images have the same properties as our global internal images. We dialectically realize them as inert copies of past readings;

they reinforce our sense of selfness and are experienced as the constituents of an ever-accessible *linguistic visual memory bank*, which serves as our personal, mobile dictionary whose linguistic images represent the spelling of each visually perceived word and the symbols of numbers.

The characteristic features of humans' capacity of speech, the clinical consequences of cerebral vascular accidents, and N. Geschwind's "disconnection syndrome,"[5] the left/right brain research by R. W. Sperry and M. S. Gazzaniga (see chap. 8), and recent MRI studies afford the following conclusions in regard to the neuronal and neural organization in the left and right cerebral hemispheres and the functional consequences of their mnemonic fusions in regard to our mental experiences.

The left hemisphere stores (1) *acoustic* engrams reflecting perceived language in Wernicke's auditory association cortex and (2) *linguistic* engrams in its visual association cortex. These acoustic and linguistic engrams are mnemonically fused by means of *intrahemispheric and interhemispheric* pathways (see fig. 1). This network underlies our capacity of expressive and receptive language.

The right hemisphere also stores acoustic engrams in its auditory association cortex but mainly those of *sounds* and *noises*, while the visual engrams stored in its association visual cortex reflect the gestalts of *global visual percepts*. The intrahemispheric mnemonic fusions between these engrams explain our ability to describe sound and sight experiences.

Interhemispheric connections. The only conceivable function of the innate existence of neural pathways between the visual association cortices of the left and right hemispheres, as shown in figure 1, is the formation of mnemonic fusions that thus connect the *mental contents* contained in the gestalts of global visual engrams stored in the right brain, with the linguistic engrams retained in the left, "speaking" brain. This interhemispheric neural network explains how we articulate our thoughts and experience various mental events that historically have been viewed as functions of the mind yet appear to be *autonomously* occurring neurophysiological events. When we happen to *read* somewhere the name John, we cannot help

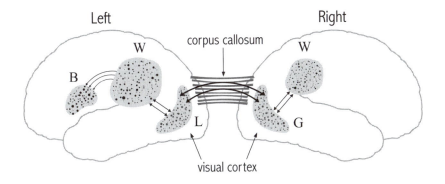

B = Broca speech center

W = Wernicke's auditory association area

L = Visual association area (linguistic gestalts)

G = Visual association area (global and partial gestalts)

Fig. 1. Interhemispheric and intrahemispheric connections between visual and auditory memory

thinking (i.e., internally seeing our internal gestalt) of our good friend John. When we happen to "run into" John at some event, we instantaneously greet him by his name without any mental effort. Equally swiftly and effortlessly, it then occurs to us that we had not seen him for two months.

This capacity for remembering temporal details of past events reflects the digital variant of linguistic engrams that are compositions of numbers reflecting day, month, year, telephone numbers, birth dates, and such. These linguistic engrams appear to be also incorporated in the interhemispheric mnemonic fusions between descriptive engrams and global engrams.

Provided normal developmental and functional circumstances, all human beings become aware of the interconnectedness of their memories. This awareness is evident from the frequently used practice when one is unable to retrieve the memory of some past experience, or some specific knowledge or the time of its occurrence, then slowly screens one's linguistic memory bank so to "promote" the activation of associated global gestalts, as we did when we remembered our briefcase in the car or as we do when conducting internal dialogues to review past experiences to form plans for future activities.

As mentioned, linguistic engrams have the same properties as global visual engrams, such as our capacity to actualize selected engrams. This capacity enables us to memorize emotional and somatoceptive experiences that cannot be mnemonically reproduced in and of themselves, such as the flavor of our favorite food, a disturbing painful physical or sad experience, the exhilarating sight of a breathtaking scenery, or the unforgettable performance of that piano concert. During our developmental years, we have come to verbally describe these empirical qualities usually by environmental verbal input. These descriptions are registered by virtue of our linguistic and digital engrams, which thus secure the memories of these qualities and our ability to later "talk about them."

Our capacity to independently actualize selected linguistic engrams leads to another and most critical intellectual function: *our ability to conceptualize*. We mentally bind objects, activities, or just thoughts that share a common denominator into one representational concept, such as the concept of flowers or the weather. This function also explains how we develop dialectical concepts of opposing yet inextricable memories of such experiences as nights and days, memory and perception, self and nonself.

IMPLICATIONS

All foregoing discussions lead to the suggestion that our capacity of cognition is not a function of the brain or a permanently acquired function of the mind, but an empirical epiphenomenon experienced as a natural consequence of the dialectical qualities of our internal images and visual percepts.

Because our sense of cognition can come about only when we

experience the qualities of selfness and nonself, while our notions of the latter qualities cannot be realized as such without our experiencing a sense of cognition, we may conclude that our sense of cognition and our notions of self and nonself constitute an inextricable dialectical triad.

Because the realization of this dialectical triad is contingent upon the simultaneous occurrences of internal images and visual percepts, we may further conclude that our capacity of cognition and our awareness of selfness and nonself are, throughout life, in a perpetual state of development.

These conclusions combined clarify another psychological quandary that is as old as the mystery of the mind: the phenomenon of *consciousness*. While this phenomenon is usually conceived to be a function of the mind, it represents the ultimate exposition of the requisite continuity of human's epistemological awareness of the selfness of one's psychological and physical existence and functions, as opposed to the nonself world out there.

The dialectical triad also satisfies Kant's demand for proof that objects exist outside ourselves: *Objects exist out there because their images are in the mind of the beholder.*

EXPERIMENTAL AND CLINICAL EVIDENCE

If the postulates presented above are correct, one should expect that if the simultaneous experiences of internal images and actual visual percepts are disrupted, our empirical dialectical triad of cognition, sense of selfness, and consciousness will disintegrate. That this indeed occurs and so lends credence to the validity of this triad of empirical experiences is substantiated by the following experimental and clinical observations.

D. O. Hebb at McGill University in Montreal deprived healthy volunteers of *all sensory input*. Within six hours, all subjects had lost their sense of self as well as their capacity for reality orientation, that is, the ability to differentiate between the *internal* origin of thoughts, memories, and ideas versus the *external* origin of visual sensory experiences. When the deprivation was continued beyond twelve hours, all subjects developed psychotic symptoms and were severely impaired in all cognitive functions.[6]

The same abnormalities are observed when the *internal* (i.e., cerebral) activation of internal images is reduced, as is the case in certain psychiatric conditions. For instance, patients suffering from endogenous depression caused by a deficiency of neurotransmitters (which are essential for the continual excitation of brain activities) usually experience sensations of "nihilism" or "depersonalization" (loss of sense of selfness), misinterpret reality, and show cognitive impairment known as "pseudodementia," so designated because it disappears when the depression lifts.

Not only are the continual and simultaneous occurrences of internal images and visual percepts essential for the formation and preservation of our self/nonself/cognitive experiences, it is also imperative that we experience ample *variations* in cognitive *content* of both global and transient gestalts by means of varying appearances and disappearances of transient objects and changes in global scenery as well. Social or perceptual monotony as experienced in solitary confinement, during solo ocean crossings, or by hapless explorers is known to have caused depersonalization and illusional or delusional interpretations of reality.

Besides the experimental and clinical evidence presented above, there is a *natural*, nightly recurring event that also substantiates the prerequisites for the simultaneous occurrences of internal images and visual percepts to generate our cognition-self-nonself triad: the phenomenon of *dreaming*. As detailed in chapter 12, dreaming can be conceived to occur as the result of activated internal images. Because visual sensory input is "shut off" during sleep, we usually experience dream content (gestalts) without a sense of selfness or sense of reality, or we even dream a past episode of our life as if it is actually happening. But once awake, we know that the dream reflected a previously experienced episode in our life.

—•—

The empirical nature of cognition highlights the fortuitous idea of historical theoreticians to designate human's internal images as *mental*, that is, *nonphysical* images, or, equally appropriate, as *mental representations* of previously experienced external events. This prompts the question: If mental representations are indeed autochthonous experiences as conceived in this chapter, then what is their relationship to the mind?

NOTES

1. G. W. Allport, *Pattern and Growth in Personality* (New York: Holt, Rinehart and Winston, 1961); J. Nash, *Developmental Psychology* (Englewood Cliffs, NJ: Prentice-Hall, 1970); L. J. Stone and J. Church, *Childhood and Adolescence* (New York: Random House, 1979).

2. S. J. Bruner, *Studies in Cognitive Growth: A Collaboration at the Center for Cognitive Studies* (New York: Wiley, 1966); J. H. Flavell, *The Developmental Psychology of Jean Piaget* (Princeton, NJ: Van Nostrand, 1964); H. G. Furth, *Piaget and Knowledge* (Englewood Cliffs, NJ: Prentice-Hall, 1969); Nash, *Developmental Psychology*; M. A. S. Pulasky, *Understanding Piaget* (New York: Harper & Row, 1980).

3. J. L. Philips, *The Origin of Intellect* (San Francisco: Freeman, 1969).

4. Quoted in E. W. Straus and E. Y. H. Natanson, *Psychiatry and Philosophy* (New York: Springer-Verlag, 1969).

5. N. Geschwind, "Brain Disease and the Mechanisms of Mind," in *Function of the Brain*, ed. C. W. Coen (Oxford: Clarendon Press, 1985), pp. 160–80.

6. P. Solomon et al., *Sensory Deprivation* (Cambridge, MA: Harvard University Press, 1961).

4

MENTAL IMAGES, MENTAL FUNCTIONS, AND THE MIND

"**P**erceiving, feeling, remembering, imagining, willing and thinking are usually said to be mental states or processes. Since there are no states or processes in themselves but only states *of* some entity and processes *in* some entity, we must ask *what* 'minds', i.e., what is the thing that perceives, feels, remembers, imagines, wills and thinks."[1]

This view of the mind as some entity that initiates and controls mental functions is a reflection of Aristotle's use of the term *psyche* to denote all mental functions that distinguish the *animate* from the *inanimate*. Aristotle included in these mental functions remembering, thinking, feeling, emotions, and perceptions. Later philosophers replaced the term *psyche* with the term *mind* to accentuate its *intellectual* activities as opposed to the *physical* features and functions of the body. This disparateness was responsible for the still-unresolved dispute between the *monistic psychophysical* theorists and the Cartesian *dualists*. Freud, in his effort to explain the dynamics of his interpretations of psychopathological conditions, divided the mind in three hypothetical structures (ego, superego, and id) and empowered them with specific mental functions. Although this may reflect his acceptance of the mind as the origin of all mental functions, Freud emphasized the hypothetical nature of these structures, as discussed in chapter 11.

A major problem with the assumed existence and functions of the mind is the lack of a clarification of its actual nature and origin despite numerous efforts throughout the long historical use of the term. Reasons for the tenacity of this problem become apparent when we apply the cerebral/empirical concept of mental images as described in the previous chapters.

First, contrary to previous efforts to conceive the nature of the mind, this concept defines what is mental and what is not. The adjective *mental* refers to the empirical, that is, *nonphysical*, notion of previously experienced visual and auditory percepts. The terms *feelings* and *perceiving* are references to *sensorial* experiences, which are *neurophysiological* events aroused by *neuronal* activities in well-defined areas of the brain, such as the association cortices and the limbic regions, which are the sources of all emotional experiences. Therefore, perceiving and feeling are not mental experiences. The fact that most mental activities are associated with emotional or somatic qualities (mnemonic or as real sensations) can be explained by the *mnemonic fusions* that are formed between visual engrams and the mnemonic storage areas of our emotional and somatic experiences and that are constantly and reciprocally reactivated during our everyday activities (see part 2).

Second, because mental images are the *carriers* of our sense of knowing and the *containers* of cognitive content by virtue of their gestalts, *they are the only conceivable "cognitive units" that make it possible to explain all our mental experiences and activities.* Only because of our mental images are we capable of assessing recurring and new visual percepts. Only by means of our mental images are we capable of memory retrieval, introspection, reading, mathematics, and future planning. Thinking is inconceivable without mental images. Aristotle concluded, "There is no thought without images." We may take that conclusion one step further: Thoughts *are* images; thinking is experiencing mental images whose gestalts determine the content of our thoughts. When we think of our home, we are experiencing images of our house, family room, or den; when we think of a friend or relative, we internally "see" images of her or his face or other physical characteristics; when the six-year-old child has become aware of the differences between the gestalts of mental images and the gestalts of actual visual percepts, she or he has begun to think. And how could we adaptively organize our everyday social and professional interactions without our mental images we form of others' reactions to our past actions and conduct?

While all these mental activities described above have traditionally been viewed as functions of the mind, the autochthonous, cerebral/empirical nature of our mental activities calls such a view into question. So does another characteristic feature of our mental experiences: During the waking states, we constantly experience a steady stream of thoughts, memories, ideas, and wishes *without having the power to volitionally initiate, interrupt, terminate, or change the velocity of the flow of our mental events.* This constant and mentally ungovernable flow of our mental experiences also indicates that our mental images are not controlled by some mental process or system such as the mind but by the only other conceivable alternative, namely, some *cerebral* process (consistent with our notion that mental images are activated neuronal engrams). Nor is it possible to conceive the other component of our capacity for cognition (our sense of having experienced before) as a product or function of the mind if we accept the proposal that our sense of cognition is a *dialectical epiphenomenon* of our simultaneous experiences of internal images and visual percepts.

In summary: the mentally ungovernable occurrences of mental images, the autochthonous dialectical nature of their cognitive component, and the unquestionable cerebral basis of their cognitive content not only explain the historical difficulties in defining the nature and origin of the mind, they also suggest a reverse approach to this problem, that is, to explore the possibility that our mental images might be the *formative elements* of that "thing" we call the mind.

We not only experience our mental images as individual events because of the specificity of their gestalts; we also experience them as components of a *conceptual conglomerate of innumerable visual mental images.* This conceptual conglomerate is the natural end result of all the features and dynamics involved in the development of our capacity of cognition, as detailed in chapter 3. I described in that chapter the formation of our right and left visual memory banks (global versus linguistic gestalts, respectively), permanently stocked with ever-accessible memories of past visual and linguistic experiences; their mnemonic fusions by means of interhemispheric, bidirectional neural pathways; and that these memory banks are continually "lit up" during the waking states. Even though we normally can experience only one given thought, idea, or wish at any given moment, the simultaneously ongoing daily experiences of recognition and awareness of object permanence, and the constant changes of visual gestalts from image to percept and vice versa, keep us perpetually aware of the permanent presence of the content of our visual and linguistic memory banks as well as their consistent (i.e., chronological) location in our memory banks. This latter experiential combination explains why we, as the sole recipients of all empirical properties of mental images, experience them as the *constituents of a conceptual entity that represents innumerable mental images* unified by a continual quality of selfness, cognition, and all the knowledge we have acquired thus far.

We also form a second conceptual conglomerate, namely, of our auditory images. Although an independent entity, it is inextricably interconnected with our experiences of global (visual) mental images and linguistic images by virtue of their reciprocal mnemonic fusions. It so enables us to verbally describe visual content, empirical, that is, nonvisible, events (such as our sense of self), and to "chronologize" the sequential formation of mental images by means of mnemonically fused verbal "markers" of time, day, week, year (see chap. 3).

Because the events described above occur during our waking states autonomously and incessantly, we experience our visual and auditory mental images as reflections of two distinctively different yet inextricable mental entities: one conceptual conglomerate of innumerable visual mental images that serve as the cornerstones of our memory and provide us with the dialectical triad of self, nonself, and sense of cognition, and another conceptual conglomerate of numerous auditory and linguistic images that enable us to identify and chronologize our visual mental images and to verbally express all other mental experiences and activities.

These two conceptual entities thus represent the storage of all memories of our visual and auditory experiences. In nearly all definitions of the mind developed throughout history, the storage and retrieval of memory are considered the fundamental characteristics of the mind. However, while the traditional definitions consider our capacity of memory as a function of the mind, the cerebral/empirical concept suggests that humans' capacity to remember is a function of our mental images, thus the product of autochthonous cerebral/empirical events. Only when visual or auditory engrams are activated and the consequent actuated images are simultaneously experienced with actual visual or auditory percepts do we, as the sole recipients of all empirical events, dialectically experience them as mental representations of previously experienced visual or auditory perceptions. Therefore, *mental representations are not functions of the mind but serve as its constituents as exemplified by our notions of the two conceptual conglomerates.*

Not only do we experience all our internal images as memories because of their concurrent sense of having experienced before; we also experience them with a sense of selfness. This inextricable combination explains why we experience the mind as a self entity and why the inextricably associated sense of cognition makes it appear if this were a function of the mind. The same is true for our sense of consciousness because it also is an inseparable component of the dialectical self, nonself, and cognitive triad (see chap. 3).

Because our awareness of mental representations is an empirical product, our concept of the mind as a conglomerate of numerous memories also is an empirical product. As an empirical concept, the mind has no substance and thus never attains the status of permanence. It can be experienced only mentally. It does not think, remember, feel, perceive, or want. Only we, as the sole recipients of all empirical events, can realize our cognitive units as the containers of knowledge and as the carriers of having experienced before. Only we feel emotional or somatic sensations that make us wish, hope, or avoid, thanks to the mnemonic fusions between emotional and somatoceptive areas and our cerebrally stored memories of certain events or our behaviors.

These mnemonic fusions enable us to clarify another apparent function of the mind. For example, when we review past experiences in preparation for future actions, we focus on selected mental images to internally "look back" at our previous actions or events, then we use the same gestalt to look forward to the anticipated results and decide whether to use or modify previous actions for our contemplated activities. These mental activities are commonly described as such mental functions as introspection, conceiving, and projecting, whereas they can be conceived as particular modes of employing our mental images by virtue of their cerebral/empirical origin, as detailed in part 2.

THE SIGNIFICANCE OF LANGUAGE

Although language has generally been considered not to play a primary role in the development of cognition,[2] the cerebral/empirical view of the nature of mental experiences would not exist without humans' linguistic capacity. Without our ability to form linguistic engrams and mnemonically fuse them with empirical events, we would not be able to mnemonically solidify and thus describe our notions of selfness, nonself, sense of having experienced before, or memories of past emotional and somatic experiences.

To substantiate this position, it is helpful to address the question: Do infrahuman species experience a mind? One might argue that we will never know because animals are not able to communicate verbally. However, this very lack of verbal communication makes it inconceivable that animals could experience any kind of mental event. As all pet owners, zookeepers, and horse trainers know, animals do recognize, do know their homestead, even know which animals and humans are their "friends" and which are not. But their actions do not indicate an "epistemological knowing" (i.e., knowing that and what they know). This skepticism is supported by the difference between the human brain and that of other species as observed during the studies by Sperry and Gazzaniga on the lateralization of cerebral functions (see chap. 9). They concluded that humans' visual perceptions of global gestalts are lateralized to the right hemisphere, and linguistic perceptions to the left hemisphere, while they did not observe such cerebral lateralization in such infra-human species as the most intelligent species of apes.

All of the above is consistent with the fact that it takes four to five years before human offspring begin to manifest the first evidence of *experiencing and purposefully employing* the constituents of the mind, that is, his or her cognitive units. During the first twelve months, the infant does not perceive objects as such but only in fragments (see chap. 15). Subsequent internalization of objects per se is succeeded by a gradual expansion to more complex internalizations by including overall global gestalts and related transient gestalts. During the ensuing developmental years, all internalizations are mnemonically fused with linguistic engrams that are only phonetic until approximately age four, when most caregivers begin to engage in showing and playing with written and printed words and figures, thus laying the foundation for the child's linguistic solidification of such empirical events as the sense of self and nonself.

Once the child is capable of responding to requests like Piaget's to compare the memory of the ball of clay against the visual percept of the sausage, he hears the word *ball* then internally sees the activated gestalt of the mnemonically fused internal visual engram. These are the experiences that bring about a sense of selfness versus the nonself visual percepts and the subsequent differentiation between internal images and visual percepts. Internal images then become mental replays of previously experienced visual percepts. Without verbal descriptions, all these experiences would just remain what they are: empirical events. Only because of our linguistic identifications do we eventually become capable of selectively searching for given mental images and so mentally replay past experiences or engaging in internal dialogues and abstract thinking.

NOTES

1. M. Bunge, *The Mind-Body Problem* (Oxford: Pergamon Press, 1980).
2. M. S. Gazzaniga, *The Social Brain* (New York: Basic Books, 1987).

PART 2

THE CEREBRAL FOUNDATION
OF MENTAL EXPERIENCES

5

PERCEPTION AND MENTAL REPRESENTATIONS

Current theories of human perceptions are based on the classifications developed by Charles Scott Sherrington in 1923.[1] Sherrington differentiated human perceptions in three systems, according to the different origins of our sensory experiences:

1. *Interoceptive* sensory experiences, which originate in the viscera and internal organs. They are presently referred to as somatoceptive perceptions.
2. *Proprioceptive* sensory experiences, which originate in the muscles and joints and convey changes in position of muscles and joints.
3. *Exteroceptive* sensory experiences, which originate at the surface of the body as a response to stimuli from our external envirorment: touch, taste, smell, temperature, and visual and auditory percepts.

Sherrington conceived these distinctions after his discoveries of the existence of specific sensory receptors in the body for the different internal and external stimuli and the network of discrete neural pathways that propagate these stimuli from the peripheral bodily areas to their corresponding sensory terminals in the brain.

Modern electrophysiology has confirmed in minute detail these early neuroanatomical notions, and Sherrington's classification still is the undisputed foundation of today's view of human perceptions.

However, Sherrington's classification does not portray an accurate account of our exteroceptive perceptions. He lumped sensations of pain, touch, temperature, taste, and smell together with our visual and auditory sensations and categorized all of them as exteroceptive percepts on the basis of his notion that all these sensory experiences originate on the surface of the body and thus inform us about our external world. However, only visual and auditory perceptions are experienced as originating in the world out there. Only these experiences deserve the designation of *exteroceptive* percepts. In contrast, our experiences of pain, touch, temperature, and smell are sensations that originate in our body and inform us of bodily experiences. These experiences are, thus, *somatoceptive* perceptions, regardless whether they are aroused by someone's touch, a mosquito bite, a bruising bump against an object, contact dermatitis, or internally induced fever. When we read a warning sign that says "wet paint," we can satisfy our curiosity whether the warning should still be in force only by touching the painted object. The stickiness we then may feel is as little an exteroceptive event as one's sexual sensory experiences, which, according to Sherrington's classification, should also be qualified as exteroceptive happenings.

Moreover, the neurophysiology of our sensations of pain, temperature, touch, and taste is (with the exception of olfaction) exactly the same as that of all other visceral and proprioceptive, that is, somatoceptive, experiences. Their stimuli originate in peripheral nociceptors, mechanoreceptors, thermoceptors, and taste buds and are propagated via sensory-specific pathways in the spinal cord to corresponding nuclei in the thalamus to be relayed to the point-to-point representations in the *sensory homunculus* situated in the parietal cortex (see fig. 2). The sensory homunculus comprises six well-defined topographic layers positioned perpendicularly to the cortical surface so that there actually are six subhomunculi, each of which is responsive to a specific somatoceptive modality. It is by virtue of this innate, topographic layout of the body in each sensory-specific lay-

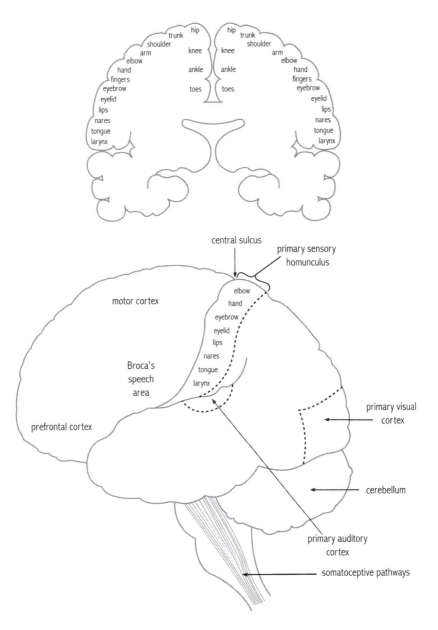

Fig. 2. Sensory homunculi

ering that we are capable of recognizing a specific somatic sensory experience *as well as the bodily location where the sensation originated.*

The fate of visual and auditory stimuli is very different from that of somatoceptive stimuli. Following their arrival at the retinas and tympanic membranes, the energies of light and sound waves are transduced into "common" neuronal stimuli, which are subsequently conducted via the optic and acoustic nerves to the primary visual and auditory cortices. The resulting activation of these cortical areas does not cause us to experience sensations of the eyes or ears; they cause us to experience shapes and forms of extraneous, nonself objects, or music or words all recognized as originating "out there." Unlike the point-to-point topographic bodily representations in the sensory homunculi, the primary visual and auditory cortices are not object-specific terminals but uncommited, neutral "screens" that make it possible to perceive the usual changes in our global gestalts, the different shapes and sizes of transient objects and their continual appearances and disappearances.

Furthermore, and most pertinent to our discussion, there is the difference in mental reproducibility between our somatoceptive experiences and our exteroceptive visual and auditory perceptions. We are able to activate visual or auditory engrams formed by our visual and auditory perceptions and so replay previous visual and auditory experiences, but we cannot under normal psychological conditions mentally reproduce our somatoceptive sensations. For example, as one thinks back to one's last visit to the dentist for the relief of a nightlong toothache, one can visualize oneself sitting in the dental chair, mouth wide open, the dentist busily exploring with his impersonal instruments, but one cannot mentally reproduce the pain experienced during that night. Another oral example: when hungry, we can visualize a steaming bowl filled with our favorite soup, but we cannot smell or taste soup until we have soup before us.

Sherrington's classification did not include our mental experiences, although such omission is perfectly understandable in light of their unknown origin in his time. As conceived in part 1, all mental events involve the internal "perception" of the gestalts of actualized visual images that we experience as a consequence of activated cerebral engrams. Therefore, mental representations (both visual and auditory) are cerebral in origin and thus can be classified as cerebroceptive experiences.

Sherrington also excluded emotional experiences, which is understandable as well because the origin of emotions was unknown until 1937, when James Papez introduced his concept of emotional circuitry. Puzzling is the fact that the general literature on perceptions and memory does not include emotional perceptions even though emotional experiences are as real as physical sensations; their origin has been established as the limbic system; and we do store their memories (see chap. 9).

Thus, if we, like Sherrington, categorize our perceptual experiences according to their origins, a more accurate classification and definition would be as follows.

1. *Exteroceptive perceptions*, which originate in our external world and are experienced as visual and auditory percepts.
2. *Somatoceptive perceptions*, which originate in our body and are experienced as nociceptive, proprioceptive, thermal, visceral, tactile, gustatory, and olfactory events.
3. *Cerebroceptive perceptions*, which originate in the visual and auditory association cortices of the brain and are experienced as visual and auditory mental representations.
4. *Emotional experiences*, which originate in different centers of the limbic system and are experienced as contentment, sadness, love, anger, fear, and such.

While the traditional classification of Sherrington has served the neurophysiologist, the neurologist, and neurosurgeon so well and so long in clinical practice, the classification proposed above has two theoretical advantages, without affecting clinical practice. First, it acknowledges the brain as the source of our mental experiences. Second, the distinction between mentally reproducible exteroceptive percepts and mentally nonreproducible somatoceptive percepts leads us to conceive two distinctively different ways in which we can perceive our body and that have significant ramnifications for all our mental experiences and mental activities.

Exteroceptive body perceptions are defined as perceptions of our body by means of our visual and auditory sensory system. The reason for qualifying our visual and auditory perceptions of our own body as exteroceptive events is that these forms of bodily perception are identical to our visual and auditory perceptions of external objects. For example, when one views one's hand, or one's face in the mirror, or listens to one's voice, one perceives from a physiological point of view each bodily part as one perceives any external source of stimulation. Like all other visual and auditory stimuli, our exteroceptive bodily stimuli are transduced at the retinas or tympanic membranes to the visual and acoustic regions in the brain. Because we are capable of mentally reproducing visual and auditory percepts after cessation of their original occurrences (which is normally not possible with our somatoceptive bodily sensations), our exteroceptive body percepts are the only bodily perceptions that result in the experience of mental representations of the body (conveniently referred to as "body images").

Somatoceptive body perceptions reflect our perceptions generated by peripheral bodily stimuli, which are conducted from sensory receptors via sensory-specific neural pathways to the sensory homunculi, as described previously, with the exception of olfactory sensations, which terminate in the olfactory bulbs.

Our awareness of all somatoceptive sensations, be it pain, touch, postural changes, thirst, or sexual experiences, is contingent upon their actual occurrence. After their cessation, these bodily sensations cannot be mentally reproduced in or of themselves. Consequently, we cannot form mental representations or body images of our somatoceptive sensations.

However, we do store memories of their occurrences. This is evident from our ability to recognize recurring sensations as pain, hunger, and a full bladder and from our capacity to remember that we experienced pleasurable or displeasurable bodily sensations in the past. If we are unable to mentally replay our somatoceptive experiences in and of themselves, how, then, can we remember that we experienced them before? This is possible by means of (1) our ability to verbally label our empirical experiences (see chap. 3) and

(2) by way of the mnemonic fusions formed between between our mentally reproducible visual and linguistic engrams and somatoceptive experiences detailed in the next chapter.

All empirical features of our somatoceptive experiences described above apply to our emotional experiences as well. Our awareness of emotions is contingent upon their actual occurrence. Emotional events cannot be mentally reexperienced, that is, mentally activated, yet we do recall having felt sad, happy, angry, or lonely in the past by virtue of the mnemonic fusions between emotional experiences and mentally reproducible exteroceptive (visual and auditory) percepts. Therefore, all further discussions and conclusions regarding the empirical and mnemonic features of our somatoceptive experiences apply to our emotional experiences as well.

NOTE

1. C. S. Sherrington, *Integrative Action of the Nervous System* (London: Yale University Press, 1923).

6

MNEMONIC FUSIONS

The concept of mnemonic fusions was introduced in 1985[1] in an effort to clarify the reciprocal and irrepressible associations between our memories of our emotional, somatoceptive, and cognitive experiences. Hearing the word *lemon* reminds us of the shape, color, and taste of the fruit; reading a letter or seeing a photograph of a dear friend or close relative arouses our memories or even feelings of fondness or love; images of past visual percepts experienced during dreams are inextricably combined with notions or even sensations of fulfilling enjoyment or nightmarish fright. To illustrate how the concept of mnemonic fusions may clarify associative memory, I use a rather remarkable manifestation of mnemonic associations: the establishment of basic trust and attachment during the first year of human life when cognitive functions have yet to be developed.

There exists a wealth of evidence to prove that the establishment of basic trust and attachment is essential for the infant's future emotional and intellectual growth. That this development must begin during the first year of life (see chaps. 5 and 19) when the infant's cognitive abilities are not even in *statu nascendi*, and the appearances of caregivers and their interactions with the infant are merely experienced as neural events, raises the obvious question: How do infants develop basic trust in and become attached to an external "object" without being capable of realizing the existence of the object?

Because the appearances of caregivers and their interactions with the infant can be experienced by the still-mindless infant only as neural events, we can address this question only in terms of the infant's exteroceptive and somatoceptive sensory experiences. Even though cognitive abilities are still years away, the neonate's behaviors soon indicate that he has begun to distinguish between the various pleasurable and displeasurable sensations evoked by the mother's appearances and her feeding, diapering, and caressing activities. His rapidly expanding preferences for and aversions to her different approaches, and his recognition of her comforting appearance or voice during moments of stress (hunger, wet diaper), afford two conclusions.

First, they indicate that the infant has formed visual and auditory memory traces (which are rudimentary engrams) of previously experienced physical features of the mother and her different activities and vocalizations during her unilateral conversations with the infant. These engrams are the infant's earliest internal representations that, when activated, enable the infant to recognize the mother's reappearances and serve as the neuronal foundations of his future mental experiences and activities. Because these future mental representations are reflections of the mother's bodily presentations, I designated them as *extraneous body images* in distinction from his later-developed images of his own bodily features as detailed in chapter 15.

Second, the infant's ability not only to recognize the mother's reappearances but also to anticipate the pleasurable or displeasurable consequences associated with her reappearances and actions indicates that he "remembers" the pleasurable or displeasurable feeling states experienced during her previous appearances. This indicates that the infant has, in addition to the formation of visual and auditory internal representations, also formed memory traces of his somatoceptive or emotional sensory experiences. However, remembering as conceived in part 1 is an impossibility during the first few years of life, and even when established, emotional and somatoceptive sensations cannot be mentally reproduced in and of themselves, not even by us adults. Therefore, we assume that the infant's anticipation of pleasurable or displeasurable experiences is inextricably linked with the extraneous body images with which he "recognizes" the mother's reappearances and actions.

Because the experiences of extraneous body images also are at this stage of development "nothing but" neural events, the infant's dual recognition of the mother and the associated somatoceptive or emotional consequenses of her intentions suggests that: whenever the infant simultaneously experiences two or more different sensory modalities, for example, an exteroceptive event (mother's appearance) and a somatoceptive or emotional event (evoked by the mother's ministrations during the appearance), not only are the "memories" of both events stored as neuronal engrams in their respective information storage areas (visual and auditory cortex and sensory homunculus), but their engrams are, as a consequence of their simultaneous precipitation, consolidated by means of neural pathways.

Based on our present knowledge of the neurophysiological properties of neural pathways in the brain (detailed momentarily), I designated the empirical results (associated memories) of the neural consolidation of given mnemonic storage areas in the brain as *mnemonic fusions*.

Because the neural pathways that underlie the occurrence of mnemonic fusions are bidirectional, the activation of a given engram (or memory) will activate the interconnected engram. Thus, whenever the mother reappears, the infant "recognizes" her appearance and actions by means of his activated matching extraneous body image, which, in turn, excites the mnemonically fused pleasurable sense of being fed and loved. (This sense is during the naive state of infancy the empirical equivalent of memory.) Mnemonic fusions thus cause the infant to "anticipate" the pleasurable and comforting consequences of the mother's reappearances. This predictability constitutes the foundation of the infant's basic trust— provided, of course, that the mother's actions toward and interactions with the infant have been consistent, of positive quality and sufficient frequency.

As a consequence of the satisfying and comforted feeling states associated with his experiences of activated extraneous body images representing the mother, the behaviorally maturing infant begins to make efforts to "solicit" the recurrences of pleasurable sensations by looking for, or staying around or clinging to, the object (mother, caregiver) that will actualize desirable extraneous body images because they promote desirable feelings. These behavioral efforts are the manifestations of *attachment*.

However, the child's cognitional realization of mnemonic fusions cannot begin before his or her development of abstract thinking, at approximately age five. Until that age, basic trust and attachment are only empirical events. The reason for having discussed the development of basic trust and attachment during the first, incogitant year of life was to illustrate that the formation of mnemonic fusions is not a cognitive product but naturally occurring, unquestionably cerebral in origin, and whose mnemonic interactions (i.e., reciprocal activations) are instantaneous, automatic, and impervious to cognitive control.

Mnemonic fusions are formed between any conceivable somatoceptive, emotional, and exteroceptive memories. Once the exteroceptive visual and auditory engrams are experienced as cognitive entities, we become aware of the existence of mnemonic fusions. But it is this very sense of cognition or having experienced before that may induce the notion that mnemonic fusions are the products of our capacity of cognition.

The notion that mnemonic fusions are natural occurrences is substantiated by two well-established phenomena observed in infrahuman species. One phenomenon was discovered by Konrad Lorenz in 1971, which he designated as imprinting.[2] Lorenz employed this term to describe the remarkable attachment that newborn birds (and many newborn mammals as well) develop immediately following hatching. Ducklings, goslings, and chicks become attached to the very first object visable, regardless whether it is the mother, a human being, a decoying object, or a match box, as long as it moves.

This attachment is apparent from such specific behaviors as chicks forever following the farmer's wife or a duckling's flying motions imitating Lorenz's butterfly strokes while swimming with him.

Lorenz concluded that many instinctive behaviors in birds and mammals do not unfold their full potential unless these behaviors are attached to the internalized "image" of an external object. Lorenz denominated the process by which "instinctive behaviors are attached to an internalized image of an external object" as *imprinting*.

The concept of imprinting has contributed significantly to the study and understanding of the environmental impact on the future behaviors of both animals and humans. If not allowed to occur during the "critical period" (which is between sixteen and twenty-four hours following hatching) by keeping, for example, a hatching egg in darkness for three days, fear and avoidance of all external objects may be the permanent consequence for the newborn. *Imprinting is "for life"; it is irreversible; it will not disappear after its establishment, even if the conspecific mother later replaces the imprinted non-specific object.*

The relevance of imprinting to the concept of mnemonic fusions lies in the fact that imprinting takes places under permanently noncognitive conditions and therefore can be understood only as the result of the formation of interneuronal connections between engrams of exteroceptive perceptions and somatoceptive or "emotional" (limbic) experiences. To further illustrate the similarities between mnemonic fusions of the noncognitive human infant and infrahuman species, I cite one example of Lorenz's fascinating observations. When the mother bird returns from her search for food and perches on the rim of the nest, the "infant" bird does not respond as if she were a stranger, which is, actually, not surprising in view of the look-alikes of birds. It is only when the mother bird begins to exhibit her usual behavior associated with feeding that the infant bird immediately starts to exhibit anticipatory behaviors associated with feeding, such as begging. This "recognition" of the mother's feeding behavior is analogous to the *dual recognition* by the human infant of the mother's appearance and activities, which we conceived as the result of mnemonic fusions between extraneous body images (which are comparable to imprints) and somatoceptive experiences.

Lorenz conceived the development of imprinting as a "self-conditioning" process that represents, of course, nature's replica of what

Pavlov experimentally produced[3] in his laboratory: *the phenomenon of conditioning.* This phenomenon also lends support to the notion that mnemonic fusions are the results of neural connections formed between simultaneously precipitated engrams of different sensory modalities in animals and humans alike. The predictability of the consistent "anticipation" of Pavlov's dog of somatoceptive sensations (reflected by salivation) when reexperiencing a given exteroceptive sensation (sound of the bell) can be explained only on the basis of acquired neural circuits established by the coupling of simultaneously precipitated engrams of somatoceptive and exteroceptive experiences.

The phenomena of imprinting and conditioning afford two conclusions. First, the formation of mnemonic fusions appears to be a *universal occurrence* in all species that possess some form of central nervous system and a visual perceptual system. Second, mnemonic fusions provide critical functions. In infrahuman species, they are indispensable for the unfolding of innate instinctive behaviors, and they serve as biological equivalents of memory comparable to the molecular concept of memory as conceived by Kandel[4] and explain the development of basic trust in and attachment to their caretakers. In addition to the latter functions, mnemonic fusions are indispensable in the development of all cognitive capacities. As detailed in chapter 3, language cannot develop without mnemonic fusions between linguistic engrams and visual engrams or without mnemonic fusions between linguistic engrams and empirical events such as selfness, nonself, and having experienced before, nor could we identify and mentally reproduce the latter notions and comparable experiences such as taste, pain, and happiness.

Both categories of visual/auditory as well as exteroceptive/somatoceptive and emotional mnemonic fusions continue to be formed throughout life while most of them are there to stay because of their neural fabric as long as the brain continues to function optimally. All mnemonic fusions show the same properties because of their neural foundation and because their underlying neural pathways are bidirectional. Thus, mnemonic fusions are reciprocal, that is, the activation of one memory activates its fused counterpart, and these activations are irrepressible. For example, we visualize food or our favorite restaurant when we feel hungry, and we irresistibly experience a surge of appetite upon the sight of a scrumptious-looking steak. A most unfortunate yet convincing example of the powerful and lasting impact of mnemonic fusions on the behaviors in humans is addiction. The well-known urge an alcoholic individual experiences upon the *sound* of tinkling ice cubes or the *sight* of a liquor bottle or when *passing a pub* is induced by activated mnemonic fusions between exteroceptive engrams and mnemonically fused somatoceptive memories. Because the automatically and instantaneously occurring urges are based on autonomous activities of permanent neuronal constructs (detailed in part 4), any form of addiction is hard to undo.

Mnemonic fusions not only are the tools of all behavioral learning; they are the determinants of our associative epistemological memory as well.

THE NEURONAL FOUNDATION OF MNEMONIC FUSIONS

Is there a way to substantiate that mnemonic fusions are based on neural pathways? An answer is available thanks to the serendipitous observations of the neurosurgeon Wilder Graves Penfield in 1940 while operating on patients suffering from intractible epilepsy. This surgery is preceded by the localization of the epileptic focus by applying small electrical currents to the suspected brain area. This procedure is performed under local anesthesia so that the patient can report changes in intellectual functions in order to avoid damage to critical parts of the brain. When Penfield stimulated areas in the temporal cortex, patients reported experiences of visual and auditory flashbacks of a dreamlike state that were associated with "eerie" feelings of familiarity. Some patients reported that ongoing activities in the operating room appeared somehow familiar, as if they had happened before or seemed to be part of a dream. When a given area was repeatedly stimulated, the experience was always identical. Penfield reacted to his observations as follows:

We have to explain how it comes that when an electrode is applied steadily to the cortex, it can cause a ganglionic complex to re-create a steadily unfolding phenomenon, a psychological phenomenon. . . . It is obvious that there is, beneath the electrode, a recording mechanism for memory of events. But the mechanisms seem to have recorded much more than the simple event. When activated, it may reproduce the emotions which activated the original experience. It seems obvious that such duplicated recording patterns can only be performed by the cerebral cortex after there has been complete coordination or integrations of all the nerve impulses that passes through both hemispheres—that is to say, that all the nerve impulses that are associated with or the result from the experience. It seems to be the integrated whole that is recorded.[5]

Penfield's interpretations did not meet the approval of more recent researchers on mental functions and the brain as indicated in Rosenfield's comprehensive review on memory concepts.[6] Indeed, it appears inconceivable that multiple cerebral stimulations of various brain areas could be integrated in one complete recording. That Penfield's single stimulation of some neural tract or some given area such as Wernicke's results in a complex mnemonic experience could be interpreted as an indication of the existence of multiple mnemonic fusions formed during the original simultaneous experience of various sensory experiences. This suggestion is supported by Geschwind's later observations of the mental deteriorations in patients whose interhemispheric connections were disrupted, which led him to conceive a "disconnexion syndrome."

Nonetheless, Penfield's research brought about a radical turn in brain research, namely, the use of physiological methods that, after a century of unsuccessful anatomical investigations, established the existence of an immense network of association fibers (see fig. 3) connecting the different cortical locations that contain the memories of specific sensorial or perceptual modalities.[7]

Ever-improving methodologies eventually established that the development of association fibers unfolds according to a meticulous time schedule already apparent in the prenatal state, indicating their functional significance. During the ninth week of the embryonic

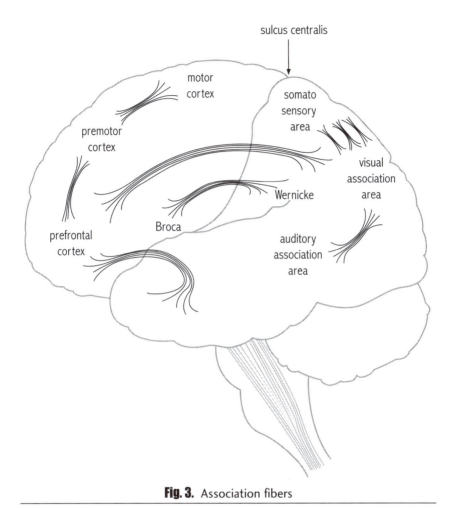

Fig. 3. Association fibers

state, association fibers begin to make their appearance, linking *interneurons* and *projective neurons* in the same cerebral hemisphere, while *commissural and callosal fibers* form connections between the corresponding cortical regions of the left and right hemispheres. Two months before birth, all neurons show a vast increase of dendrites.

At birth, the infant is equipped with two categories of association fibers: (1) innate or "wired-in" fibers that connect limbic areas with such cortical regions as the motor cortex and so provide the infant with vital reflexive behaviors during and following birth and (2) a supply of unconnected neural pathways positioned between various mnemonic storage areas prepared to form synaptic connections with the neuronal structures of engrams formed during perceptual experiences and so provide the cerebral foundations of basic trust and attachment.

Postnatal, the processes of the association neurons, interneurons, and projective neurons continue to expand but under different circumstances, that is, the awakening of metabolic activities in specific regions in the brain. These activities also unfold in a predictable temporal sequence as demonstrated with the PET studies by H. T. Chugani, M. E. Phelps, and J. C. Mazziotta.[8] During the first two months of life, neuronal activities are mainly apparent in the occipital cortex, thalamus, and sensory homunculi; then activities emerge in the motor homunculi and Broca's and Wernicke's areas; during the last six months, metabolic activities in the prefrontal cortex become increasingly apparent (see fig. 4).

At the end of the first year, the number of neurons and dendrites has increased from one thousand to one hundred thousand (possibly millions). This increase coincides with the emergence of the infant's awareness of object permanence.

The notion that the underlying neural pathways of the majority of mnemonic fusions are reciprocal is supported by the painstaking research of V. B. Mountcastle. He examined the brains of mature monkeys and established the following: (1) cortical cells are organized in vertical columns extending from the surface down through all six layers of each cortical area; (2) all neurons in each column are interconnected by uncountable but specific connections; (3) within each cortical area there are subsets of connected neurons that are connected with similar subsets in other cortical areas. Mountcastle concluded: "These connective subsets are distributed systems, each composed of modular elements in several or in many brain regions connected in both parallel and serial arrays. They form the reciprocal neuronal pathways for distributed parallel processing within the brain."[9]

—•—

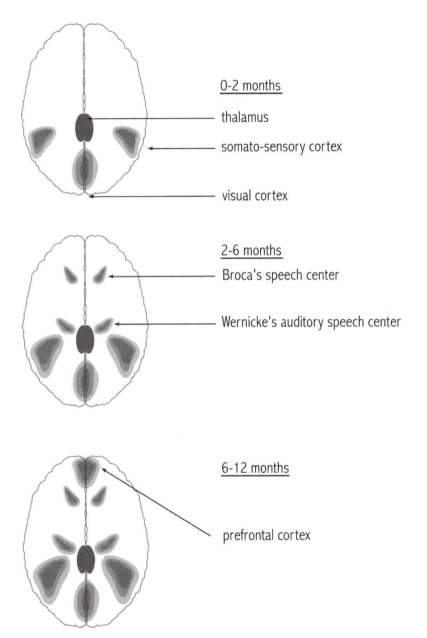

Fig. 4. Emerging metabolic activity in the human brain during the first year of life (after PET scans by Chugani et al.)

Our next obvious question is: How may we conceive the neuronal structure of the visual and auditory engrams that we presume to underlie our mental experiences?

NOTES

1. C. van der Velde, "Body Images of One's Self and of Others: Developmental and Clinical Significance," *American Journal of Psychiatry* 142, no. 5 (1985): 527–37.

2. K. Lorenz, *Studies in Animal and Human Behavior*, vol. 1 (Cambridge, MA: Harvard University Press, 1971).

3. I. P. Pavlov, *Conditioned Reflexes* (London: Clarendon, 1927).

4. E. R. Kandel, "Steps Toward a Molecular Grammar for Learning: Explorations into the Nature of Memory," in *Medicine, Science and Society*, ed. K. J. Isselbacher (New York: John Wiley, 1985).

5. W. Penfield et al., *The Mystery of the Mind* (Princeton, NJ: Princeton University Press, 1975).

6. I. Rosenfield, *The Invention of Memory* (New York: Basic Books, 1988).

7. W. S. McCullough, "The Functional Organization of the Cerebral Cortex," *Physiological Review* 24 (1944): 390–407.

8. H. T. Chugani, M. E. Phelps, and J. C. Mazziotta, "Positron Emission Tomography Study of Human Brain Functional Development," *Annals of Neurology* 22, no. 4 (1987): 487–97.

9. V. B. Mountcastle, *Handbook of Physiology: The Nervous System IV* (Bethesda, MD: American Physiological Society, 1981).

7

THE NEURONAL MATRIX OF VISUAL MENTAL REPRESENTATIONS

Our ability to mentally replay visual percepts has long been viewed as an indication that we retain imprints or engrams of our visual experiences. That visual engrams or codes are stored in the brain is evident from the occurrence of mental images when the temporal cortex is stimulated, as discussed, from the accelarated firing in cortical areas during visual remembering with PET scans and from the loss of visual recognition of objects following lesions in the visual association areas.[1] Furthermore, C. G. Gross reported the reflection of a human face in the right parietal lobe during MRI studies, while others reported the visualization of words and numbers in the left angular gyrus, the auditory association cortex.

This evidence notwithstanding, how engrams are formed, stored, and actuated into mental images continue to remain unresolved issues. These issues are related to a far more fundamental problem: the physiology of visual perception. D. H. Hubel and T. N. Wiesel,[2] Von der Heidt, Peterhansen, and P. Fries and S. Zeki have established during the last three deades that the brain's processing of visual information is, unlike its processing of other sensory modalities, not a straightforward periphery-to-cerebral terminal event. Visual stimuli are transmitted via the optic nerves from the retina to the lateral geniculate bodies (see fig. 5), where they are seg-

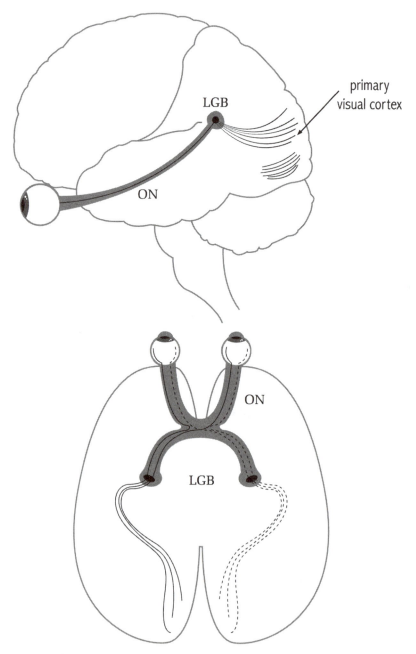

Fig. 5. LGB = lateral geniculate body; ON = optic nerve

regrated into four different pathways: one for color, one for movement, and two for form, each terminating in separate though neurally interconnected areas. This subspecialized processing raises the question whether, and if so how, the segregrated stimuli are reintegrated into one "masterpercept." This still-unresolved issue explains why it has not been possible to answer the question how the brain retains memories of visual percepts.

These obscurities led to worldwide efforts to explain human's capacity of visual memory by means of computermodels and "artificial networks."[3] Although ingeniously conceived, none of these models address the fundamental aspect of the *nature* of our sense of cognition or explain our *accessibility* to our ever-ready internal visual memory bank or our capacity of assessment of visual perceptions, recurring or new ones. Moreover, even if visual percepts are encoded in digitalized modes, we then have to explain the mechanics of translating these modes into our experiences of internal images whose gestalts replicate the gestalts of the original visual percepts. Furthermore, we cannot ignore the following.

Chapter 5 described the amazingly organized point-to-point topographic representation of our body in the parietal lobes that forms the sensory homunculus. A similar topographic arrangement characterizes the neurocellular architecture of the primary visual cortices in the left and right occipital lobes. Each primary visual cortical area is a neuronal representation of each retina divided by the left and right optic nerves. Each optic nerve contains one million fibers, half of which connect the lateral half of the retina with the ipsilateral visual cortex, and the remaining fibers connect the medial half of the retina with the contralateral visual cortex (see fig. 5).

Adjacent to and connected with the primary visual cortex lie the secondary and tertiary visual cortices. They also have a retinotopic structure. Their functions are believed to be the perception of shape and color. There are at least nine additional visual association areas, also retinotopically structured, whose functions are as yet unknown.

The functional purpose of the retinotopic organization in the primary visual cortex is diametrically opposed to the purpose of the somatotopic structure of the sensory homunculus. The somatotopic arrangement of the latter assures our consistent and precise bodily localization of somatoceptive events, whereas the retinotopic cytoarchitecture of the visual cortex enables us to perceive any external object of any size or shape or position, including every change in its appearance or spatial location. It further enables us to distinguish the two components in any given visual percept, that is, global and transient gestalts.

This retinotopic structure permits three conclusions pertinent to our current disucssion. First, the cortical point-to-point* representations of the retina indicate that the entire retina is represented in the visual cortex. Therefore, all visual percepts occupy the exact neuronal area in the primary visual cortex.

Second, the cortical representations of retinal images suggest the possiblity that seeing is experiencing excitations of the primary visual cortex, causing us to experience a gestalt whose content is determined by the particular configuration of excited neurons according to the stimulation of the retina.

Third, from the way we cognitively experience mental representations (having experienced before), as well as our constant experiencing (during the waking state), the existence of our lit-up visual memory bank (see chap. 10) indicates the existence of a neuronal matrix of our mental representations, which also explains the occurrence of dreaming during our mentally inactive states when we are asleep.

All of the above is further supported by this example, employed in part 1: We are halfway to the office when we are forced to take a detour on account of some road repair. When we spotted the detour sign, we also remembered that last night on our way home we noticed the road sign announcing that the repair would start to day. This recall also included the time of observation (the night before), indicating the individual existence of mental representations and confirming the nature of recognition conceived in chapter 1: "the experiential consequence of the simultaneous experience of a visual percept and its matching internal image."

---

*Some retino-cortical connections are not exact linear point-to-point connections but point-to-"field of neurons."

Since there are no images (or mental representations) without gestalts (meaning), I utilize the cortical organization as discussed above to suggest that visual engrams are point-to-point neuronal fascimiles of the original neuronal pattern of images on the retina, stored as is, thus available for immediate activation and, when activated, causing us to "see" an image as if each engram serves as its own "projection screen." If an engram is activited during the perception of its recurring original visual percept, we experience the percept as having experienced before. If an engram is activated in the absence of its original visual percept, the resulting image is experienced as an independent mental representation, for example, a thought, memory, or idea.

I further hypothesize that the matrix of each visual engram is localized in the visual association cortex, according to Minsky, and consists of a "neuronal sheet," a single-layered part of an enormous field of neuronal sheets in the neuronal columns that make up the visual association cortex. Their sequential formation and permanent storage explains our awareness of the different chronology of the original occurrences of cognitive experiences.

The views presented above also clarify a number of naturally occurring psychological events:

- the continually activated visual memory banks explain our ever-accessibility to our stored memories
- our awareness of having experienced a given event before
- our awareness of having met a given individual numerous times
- our sense of time (there is no cerebral function for our sense of time)
- the experience of a flashback of an entire life during near-death experiences or when about to slide into coma during anesthesia
- the many different opinions we have about other individuals combined with the awareness of their ephemeral physiognomy and attitudes

Finally, and most supportive of the notion that visual mental representations are reflections of specific neuronal engrams, are the mnemonic fusions we form between visual (pictorial) memories in the right hemisphere (for example, flowers) with auditory (linguistic) engrams in the left hemisphere that enable us to describe a rose, hyancinth, or azalea. This capacity of categorization would not exist without the continual availability of individually different mental gestalts.

SOLIDIFICATION OF VISUAL ENGRAMS

How is the initial imprint of each visual percept on a neuronal sheet "consolidated" into a permanent visual engram? Any effort to conceive an answer to this question must take into account a special requirement: It should explain not only how we permanently conserve the neuronal configuration that makes up the engram-gestalt, but how the engram still remains excitable to be actuated into a permanent mental image yet still is capable of forming mnemonic fusions with other forms of memories. In other words, the neurons of visual engrams must remain biologically active. Owing to the fascinating research by G. E. Edelman,[4] such capability appears to be a natural property of two specific categories of cells.

During his search for the mechanisms by which biological organs attain their characteristic physical shapes during embryogenesis (for example, a chicken's feathers), Edelman[5] discovered the existence of *cell and surface adhesion molecules* (CAMs). These molecules are glycoproteins situated at cell membranes and are found in the liver and in nervous tissues and hence referred to as L-CAMs and N-CAMs, respectively. The former "cement" cells that contain the same L-glycoprotein; the latter bind only nerve cells. CAMs are genetically determined and thus part of the biological organization of organisms.

The adhesive properties of N-CAMs appear to be the natural answer to the question of how we may conceive the workings of the neuronal plasticity in the visual association cortex. It is conceivable that the neurons in this cerebral area remain in an embryonic, uncommitted, nonspecific state until activated during a visual percept, at which point N-CAMs perform their cementing duties and create the neuronal morphology that determines the gestalt of the eventual internal image. Since N-CAMs do not interfere with cellular activities, the consolidated engrams remain biologically active and thus excitable.

STORAGE CAPACITY

If we indeed form an engram of every visual percept we experience, the number of engrams to be formed and stored throughout life will be astronomical. M. Hunt estimated that the lifetime capacity of the average human memory is 100 trillion bits.[6] J. Von Neuman[7] put this figure at 2.8 times that, which is 280 quintillion.

Does the brain have such storage capacity? Although it is not possible to answer this question at present, that the brain has an enormous storage potential is unquestionable. Because of the convolutions of the brain's surface, this potential is much larger than its appearance suggests. One measure of the brain's storage capacity is its neuronal density. It is generally believed that the cerebral cortex contains between 15 and 25 billion neurons, although some investigators have suggested a number as high as 100 billion.

Do we store the same visual engrams in both the right and left hemisphere?

NOTES

1. H. T. Chugani, M. E. Phelps, and J. C. Mazziotta, "Positron Emission Tomography Study of Human Brain Functional Development," *Annals of Neurology* 22, no. 4 (1987): 487–97; D. M. Kaufman, *Clinical Neurology for Psychiatrists*, 3rd ed. (Philadelphia: W. B. Saunders, 1990); E. R. Kandel and J. H. Schwartz, eds., *Principles of Neural Science* (New York, Elsevier, 1988).

2. D. H. Hubel, *Eye, Brain and Vision* (New York: Scientific American Library/Freeman, 1988).

3. H. Gardner, *The Mind's New Science: A History of the Cognitive Revolution* (New York: Basic Books, 1985); P. N. Johnson-Laird, "Propositional Representations, Procedural Semantics, and Mental Models," in *Parallel Distributed Processing*, 2 vols., ed. D. E. Rumelhart et al. (Cambridge, MA: MIT Press, 1988); D. E. Rumelhart et al., *Parallel Distributed Processing*, 2 vols. (Cambridge, MA: MIT Press, 1988); R. N. Shepard and L. A. Cooper, *Images and Their Transformations* (Cambridge, MA: MIT Press, 1982); S. Pinker, *How the Mind Works* (New York: Norton, 1999); G. E. Edelman, *Neural Darwinism: The Theory of Neuronal Group Selection* (New York: Basic Books, 1987).

4. Edelman, *Neural Darwinism.*

5. G. E. Edelman, *Topobiology* (New York: Basic Books, 1988).

6. M. Hunt, *The Universe Within* (New York: Simon & Schuster, 1982).

7. J. Von Neumann, *The Computer and the Brain* (New Haven, CT: Yale University Press, 1958).

8

LEFT AND RIGHT VISUAL MENTAL REPRESENTATIONS

In 1960 Sperry and Gazzaniga embarked upon a series of studies with patients whose uncontrollable epilepsy were reasons to perform as a last therapeutic resort a neurosurgical procedure designated as callosotomy, which aims at the severance of the interhemispheric neural connections that run through the corpus callosum, thus halting the spreading of seizures from one hemisphere to the other. Sperry and Gazzaniga examined the mental abilities of these patients postsurgery, now functioning with independent hemispheres.[1]

Although all patients superficially appeared to be mentally functioning efficiently, special testing procedures showed otherwise. The researchers took advantage of the fact that the right halves of both retinas are connected with the right visual cortex, and the left retinal halves are connected with the left visual cortex so that one-half of our visual fields are visualized in the left occipital lobe and the other half in the right occipital lobe (see fig. 5, p. 82). By blocking one-half of the visual field, it was possible to examine the mental functions associated with visual perception of each hemisphere in isolation. They discovered that in right-handed patients, linguistic capacity as well as that of reading, writing, and arithmetic, is localized in the left hemisphere. In contrast, the left hemisphere appeared incapable of visually recognizing objects. This latter capacity appeared to be the monopoly of the right hemisphere, which also appeared capable of recognizing emotional aspects in the appearances and voices of others. Because of its "superiority" in intellectual functions, the "speaking" left brain was designated as the dominant, conscious hemisphere.

Continued research with subjects whose brains were intact eventually led Sperry and Gazzaniga to conclude that the "lateralization" of mental functions is a physiological phenomenon as illustrated below. They eventually concluded that even under normal conditions the left and right brain are designated to perform different mental functions as follows:[2]

Dominant hemisphere	Nondominant hemisphere
intellect	emotions
speech	spatial perception
reading, writing	visual recognition of objects
naming objects	metaphors
musical ability	–
arithmetic	–
consciousness	unconsciousness
long-term memory	short-term memory

While this left/right differentiation described above has been universally accepted,[3] it begs the question: How is one to explain the differences in *mental experiences* in terms of left and right *cerebral functions*? To credit the left brain as the origin of consciousness assumes that consciousness is a cerebral product. Such assumption should be accompanied by a valid explanation in light of the unresolved issues surrounding the nature and origin of mental functions as discussed in the introduction. According to the dialectical concept of the mind, mental experiences are not functions of the brain or the mind but empirical events that result in the empirical triad of cognition, self, and nonself, and this triad explains the experience we have come to refer to as consciousness. The fact that our capacity of verbal communication is localized in the left brain (in 90 percent of normally functioning right- or left-handed individuals) explains why the left brain appears to be the dominant, intellectual cerebral hemisphere. However, the experience of the dialectical triad is contingent upon the simultaneous experience of the global gestalts of both internal images and visual percepts, and this experience is possible only by virtue of the right brain, as is apparent form the list above.

Therefore, before accepting the notion that the left hemisphere is dominant over the right hemisphere, we should deal with several questions. Is there an explanation for this selective "localization" of our mental functions? Do we really store long-term memory in the left brain and short-term memory in the right? Do we actually experience consciousness with the left hemisphere, or does it only appear that way because of the fact that our ability to verbally describe is possible only with the left brain? These questions cannot be addressed without discussing how we may conceive the cerebral foundation of auditory mental representations and their role in our linguistic capacity.

NOTES

1. R. W. Sperry, "Lateral Specialization in the Surgically Separated Hemisphere," in *The Neurosciences: Third Study Program*, ed. F. Schmitt and F. G. Worden (Cambridge, MA: MIT Press, 1974).

2. Ibid.

3. S. P. Springer and G. Deutsch, *Left Brain, Right Brain*, 2nd ed. (San Francisco: W. H. Freeman, 1985).

9

THE NEURAL NETWORK OF LANGUAGE

Our capacity of language is characterized by two mind-boggling features: (1) our *instantaneous* and *effortless* recognition of spoken or written words and their meaning and (2) our ability to convert our feelings, knowledge, and opinions into verbal descriptions without the assistance of a visible dictionary.

While it may appear obvious that the acquisition of language is first and foremost a matter of auditory perception, it is argued in this chapter that the processes by which we cerebrally store words, their spelling, and their connotations, and the process by which we mentally reproduce them, involve a complex neural network of the memories of both exteroceptive sensory modalities, that is, visual and auditory perception.

The vibrations of the tympanic membranes caused by acoustic stimuli are transmitted to the hair cells in the organ of Corti, which is located in the cochlea in the middle ear. Hair cells function as mechano-receptors that transduce acoustic stimuli into "ordinary" neural impulses, which are transmitted by the thirty thousand fibers that make up the acoustic nerve to the *medial geniculate bodies* (MGB), which are, most appropriately, situated in the posterior part of the thalamus adjacent to the *lateral geniculate bodies*, which are the relay stations for visual stimuli (see fig. 5, p. 82). The acoustic fibers then partially separate to radiate to the *primary auditory cortex* in the supra-posterior temporal lobes, where actual hearing takes place, and to at least five association cortical areas that lie in the immediate vicinity of the primary auditory cortex. This separating radiation is identical to that described in chapter 7.

The medial geniculate bodies and *all* auditory cortical areas are *tonotopically* organized, that is, by point-to-point connections with the hair cells in the organ of Corti, so that each acoustic imprint in every auditory cortical region represents a neuronal replica of the original acoustic percept in the cochlea (analogous to the retino-topic facsimiles in the visual association cortical areas). This replication is further secured by the fact that each of the acoustic fibers that form the point-to-point connections between Corti and the auditory cortices carries a characteristic frequency.[1] Consequently, the auditory engrams formed in the auditory association cortex are not actual "imprints" but originate as excitations of a specific tonotopic profile that is identical to the original assembly of stimulated hair cells and is solidified as such by Edelman's N-CAMs, analogous to the consolidation of visual engrams as described in chapter 7.

The *cortical association area for acoustic memory* was identified by Carl Wernicke in 1876 as lying below and adjacent to the primary auditory cortex (see fig. 6). He conceived it to be the cortical area "where the meaning of language is stored" because a lesion in this area (such as a hemorrhage) leads to the inability to *comprehend* language (usually described as sensory or receptive aphasia). This suggests that "Wernicke's area" is the region where auditory engrams are formed and stored and thus constitutes our "auditory memory bank." Wernicke's observations further disclosed that this auditory memory bank exists in the majority of patients studied only in the left hemisphere.

Auditory engrams can be distinguished in three different categories: as reflections of momentary sounds or noises, music, and verbal communication.

Momentary Sounds. Thunder, the ring of a telephone, the neighing of a horse, and the plaintive cry of seagulls leave us with auditory memories whose underlying engrams can be conceived as small assemblies of solidified tonotopical neuronal profiles.

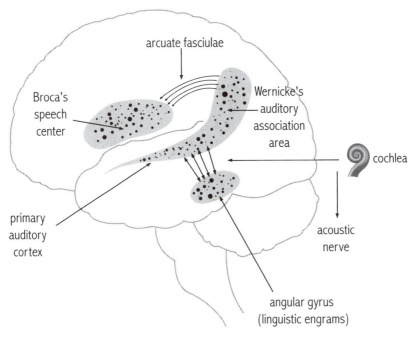

Fig. 6. Speech pathways

Music. Whether we hum a popular tune, whistle Beethoven's Fifth, or join others in singing the national anthem, we conceivably employ a given assembly of tonotopic neuronal profiles that are, like any kind of engram, *consolidated and stored in the sequence of the temporal occurrence of the original acoustic stimuli.* This is evident from the fact that we normally begin at the beginning and end at the end of our musical mental replays. Although I am aware that the use of concrete or mundane analogies in neuroscientific narrations is generally frowned upon, the temptation is too strong not to mention the analogy of our musical neuronal sheets with the "tonotopic" imprints of the pianolo rolls used to produce music with the now-antiquated player piano.

Language. Language develops in two phases. It begins during infancy (the Latin word *infant* means speechless) as phonetic communications by means of "speech sounds," which the infant internalizes as auditory engrams in Wernicke's area. These engrams are mnemonically fused with simultaneously formed visual engrams of toys, foods, mother's appearances, and activities as indicated by PET scans (see chap. 6). These mnemonic fusions enable the growing infant to name toys and foods or say "bye-bye" while waving a hand, even though epistemological know-how is still several years away.

The second phase begins between the ages of four and six years (depending upon environmental didactic input), when the child begins to also collect internal images of *visual percepts of words* that are mnemonically fused with speech sounds. Phonetic communication then becomes language as we adults experience and utilize it as follows.

Words are compositions of given sets of printed or written letters in *linear* sequence. Thus, the word *word* is only *word* when we read, that is, *see*, it as w-o-r-d. In any other order of letters, or in any other geometric position, such as $d^o r_w$, it no longer is a word. This condition also applies to words composed of permanently consolidated syllables: lin-guis-tic, phi-lo-so-phy, per-spi-ca-cious. Such isolated syllables as tic, guis, or lin do not constitute words. Once solidified by Edelman's N-CAMs, words retain their individual linear identity in sentences because they are separated by gaps. Noam Chomsky and M. Hallen have shown that we do not read sentences "in one piece"; we read every word in a sentence separately, even though we are usually unaware of such separation.[2]

Words thus represent a specific category of visual percepts that may be denominated as *linguistic visual percepts*, and their mental replays may be referred to as *linguistic internal images*. Because their gestalts determine the spelling of words, they are indispensable instruments for the development and utilization of language.

In most human beings, the cerebral engrams that underlie our linguistic internal images are not stored in the general visual memory banks, as discussed in chapter 7, but *completely occupy the visual association area in the left hemisphere*, thus forming an exclusively linguistic visual memory bank to serve, as it were, as a biological dictionary. Wernicke identified this visual association area as the *angular gyrus*, which is area number twenty-three in Brodman's brain map and the anatomical counterpart of the *general* visual memory bank in the comparable region in the right hemisphere as discussed in chapter 7.

The angular gyrus also lies below Wernicke's area, with which it is connected by reciprocal neural pathways, indicating the potential for forming mnemonic fusions between the sounds of words and their articulation. The functional significance of these mnemonic fusions is apparent from W. Penfield's investigations of human speech and brain mechanisms during neurosurgical operations.[3] Patients were asked to name an insect shown on a card while Penfield electrically inhibited various areas in Wernicke's area and the angular gyrus. When a certain point in the angular gyrus was inhibited, patients were unable to produce the correct name "butterfly" and used instead the name "moth." Immediately following the removal of the electrode, patients called the name butterfly and explained that they were momentarily unable to produce the correct name and chose the word moth "as being the closest to the picture."

Naturally, Penfield's experimentations included Broca's speech center, so named because Pierre-Paul Broca identified this region in 1861 following his observation of the loss of speech caused by a hemorrhage in that area of the brain. Broca's speech center is also located in the left hemisphere in 90 percent of all humans studied. It lies in the posterior part of the frontal lobe adjacent to the motor cortex. In fact, Broca's center itself is a motor cortex that innervates the facial muscles involved in speech. It is connected with Wernicke's area by the *fasciculus arcuata* (see fig. 6), which carries one-way neural fibers that, we may assume, convey the neuronal profiles of auditory engrams by "modeling" motor templates of the facial speech muscles and so determines word pronunciation and articulation concordant with the intonational profiles of the auditory engrams stored in Wernicke's area. When Penfield inhibited Broca's area, patients later explained that they were aware of the name butterfly but could not verbalize it. When Penfield electrically interrupted the fasciculus arcuata, patients showed a fluent "conduction aphasia."

THE MEANING OF WORDS

What exactly might Wernicke have meant when he described Wernicke's area as the cortical region "where the meaning of language is stored"? What is the meaning of our auditory perceptions and our auditory mental replays? Meaning reflects cognitive "content." Auditory engrams do not have gestalts thus do not enable us to describe the meaning of a given musical composition, a birth date, or the historical events during the years 1940–1945. The meaning of the word *furniture*, in contrast, is simple and clear: We associate the word with the contents, that is, gestalts of our visual internal images we have of chairs, a desk, or table. This word/content association is a reflection of the earlier-mentioned set of mnemonic fusions, namely, *between the linguistic engrams in the left hemisphere and the visual global gestalts in the right hemisphere.*

The interhemispheric neural tracts underlying these mnemonic fusions run through the posterior portion of the corpus callosum (see fig. 1, p. 45). Lesions in this portion of the corpus callosum result in "disconnection syndromes" described by E. A. Weinstein and R. F. Friedland, N. Geschwind and B. J. Freeman, and E. Goodglass and H. Kaplan.[4]

While the concept of mnemonic fusions is relatively new, I should mention that their formation between Wernicke's area, the linguistic visual memory bank, and the general visual memory bank has been unwittingly practiced throughout the world by elementary school teachers for over a century. Based on many years of predictable success, they present to first graders the pictures of Dick, Jane, and Spot and have them simultaneously loudly articulate the underlying corresponding words, thus precipitating permanent mnemonic fusions between given sounds and sights. Another example of the permanent effects of mnemonic fusions are the difficulties speech therapists have in modifying the motor templates in Broca's speech center of an individual with a dialect or a foreign accent, especially at advanced ages.

Finally, the last set of mnemonic fusions: the reciprocal neural connnections between the limbic system and auditory engrams. These connections enable us to remember past *empirical* events such as emotions, somatoceptive experiences, and such conceptual notions as our sense of self, nonself, and consciousness (see part 1), none of which can be mnemonically stored or mentally reproduced because of their experiential nature. Their simultaneous occurrences with the environmentally derived descriptions make it possible to remember later their occurrences by means of our linguistic engrams (see chap. 5). As described in the section about "having experienced before" in chapter 3, we also store dates and times whose linear structures are also stored in the linguistic visual memory bank and enable us to remember the chronology of their experiences.

CEREBRAL LATERALIZATION

The complete "lateralization" of our auditory memory bank, our linguistic visual memory bank, and Broca's speech center in the left brain confirms and explains the findings of Sperry and Gazzaniga listed in the previous chapter, although one might take exception with regard to the inclusion of *consciousness* and *intellect*. Consciousness as conceived in part 1 of this volume is an *empirical epiphenomenon* that cannot be localized as a function in the brain. While intellect can be verbalized only with the left brain, the brunt of our general knowledge is stored in the right visual memory bank. Furthermore, the intelligent utilization of that knowledge—as in conceptualizing or planning—is a function of the right prefrontal cortex as discussed in chapter 10.

The cause of cerebral lateralization has yet to be established. Cerebral dominance has been implicated on the basis of the natural asymmetry of the brain, which is apparent during pregnancy from the thirty-first week on. Skull studies have indicated that cerebral dominance has existed for at least three hundred thousand years. The fact that the left brain is usually larger in right-handed people offers no clarification. Efforts to establish a correlation between handedness by using the Wada test* showed that 90 percent of right-handed

---

*The Wada test is a procedure used in neurosurgery to determine on which side of an individual's brain the capacity for language is located by injecting sodium amytal in the left or right carotid artery, which provides the blood supply for the ipsilateral side of the brain. This injection causes a temporary loss of speech.

humans employ their left brain for language; so do 60 percent of the left-handers; while the remaining 40 percent of left-handers use both hemispheres. While handedness is believed to be genetic in origin,[5] language is not. Right-handed children who undergo a left hemispherectomy (usually for a brain tumor) still develop full capacity of speech if this surgery takes place before the age of ten.

I wonder whether we might consider the following physiological possibility based on the prerequisite involvement of internal visual images in language. In the English and other European languages, reading, writing, and spelling proceed from left to right. Consequently, the left lateral halves of both retinae are predominantly involved during reading and writing, so that our linguistic visual perceptions are mainly, if not conclusively, processed in the left hemisphere and thus lateralize the formation of the linguistic visual memory bank in the left angular gyrus. This explanation is consistent with the fact that 40 percent of left-handers (who use right and left visual fields equally) use both hemispheres for language.

It is conceivable that, as a matter of anatomical proximity and/or biological economy, as well as the existence of innate neural pathways, the linguistic visual memory bank forms mnemonic fusions only with the ipsilateral and neighboring Wernicke's area and Broca's speech center, which explains the lateralization of auditory memory and Broca's speech center to the left.

However, the significance of cerebral "dominance" is relativized by the fact that our visual and auditory perceptions and their memories are equally indispensable for humans' mental functions. The former inform us about the happenings in the world around us; the latter enable us to communicate our inner feelings and thoughts and to understand the feelings and thoughts of others.

What makes us think, move, talk, and listen? These are the topics of the next chapter.

NOTES

1. J. Lauter et al., "Tonotopic Organization in Human Auditory Cortex Revealed by Positron Emission Tomography," *Hearing Research* 20 (1985): 199–205.

2. N. Chomsky and M. Hallen, *The Sound Pattern of English* (New York: Harper & Row, 1968).

3. W. Penfield and L. Roberts, *Speed and Brain Mechanisms* (Princeton, NJ: Princeton University Press, 1959).

4. N. Geschwind, "Brain Disease and Mechanism of Mind," in *Function of the Brain*, ed. C. W. Coen (Oxford: Claraendon Press, 1985), pp. 160–80.

5. R. L. Gregory and O. L. Zangwill, eds., *The Oxford Companion to the Mind* (Oxford: Oxford University Press, 1987).

10

ACTUALIZATION OF MENTAL REPRESENTATIONS

There are two schools of thought on the initiation of brain activities in general. Bunge referred to them as the *causal* and as the *autogenic* views.[1] Advocates of the causal school suggest that all CNS activities are caused by extracerebral stimuli; supporters of the autogenic school assume that all brain activities are generated within the brain.

According to the classification of humans' perceptual and sensorial experiences advanced in chapter 5, both views are valid. Our exteroceptive visual and auditory experiences originate extraneously; our somatoceptive experiences originate in the body; our emotional sensations originate in the limbic system; our experiences of mental representations originate in the visual and auditory association cortices as activated internal engrams.

Reproducing mental representations is synonymous with actualizing visual mental images, which is akin to the mental function of "recall." The act of recall must begin with the activation of visual engrams because their gestalts provide the content without which we cannot experience our sense of cognition. To explore the dynamics of engram activation, we first need to qualify how we use the term *activation* in light of the similarities between our three modes of cognition as conceived in chapter 1, which are: recognition, its derivative object permanence awareness, and cognition.

A convenient starting point to illustrate their similarities and their differences is our morning awakening, when our daily mental activities return in full force. From the very moment we are awake, we recognize our familiar environment, then rise and begin our morning routine while moving from room to room flawlessly guided by our awareness of object permanence. The fact that recognition and object permanence awareness are autonomous, instantaneous, and irresistible occurrences (because they result from our simultaneous experiences of identical or similar gestalts of internal images and visual percepts) indicates that both our visual and auditory *memory banks* are "lit up."

This illumination should not be construed as the activation of specific visual engrams. It reflects the work of the *reticular activating system* (RAS), which is located in the brain stem (see fig. 2, p. 63). With the same predictability of the daily rising and setting of the sun, so does the RAS diurnally turn on and off the resting potential of all cortical regions in the brain, as is observable from the voltage changes on electroencephalograms and from the differences between the darkness of internal images during dreams versus the brighter internal images during wakefulness. Thus, the RAS affects the brain in its entirety and in all species that possess a central nervous system. For example, experimental stimulation of the RAS in infrahuman species causes hyperalertness; lesions in the reticular region of the brain stem of humans and animals result in coma and complete paralysis.

Besides the "passive" occurrences of recognition and object permanence awareness, we also experience a perpetual stream of thoughts, memories, ideas, and wishes whose contents usually are unrelated to the contents of our simultaneous experiences of recognition. We experience these *independent* (see chap. 1) mental representations without having the power to volitionally terminate, interrupt, or change the velocity of the flow of these mental events. This *constant and mentally ungovernable* flow of mental experiences indicates that these independent visual mental representations are not actualized by a mental process or mental function but by the only possible alternative: some *cerebral* source or process. Although we are not capable of interrupting this natural stream of mental experiences, we do possess a certain control over the *contents* of our mental events, namely, we can "hold on" to a given thought, "search" for a particular memory or idea, or concentrate on a mathematical problem. These are the mental experiences whose origin of actualization we wish to identify.

Such an effort should include an explanation of another characteristic of our mental events: we normally experience only one thought, one memory, *thus only one visual mental representation at any time, yet the contents of our successive thoughts usually are coherent and directed toward a given goal*, suggesting the existence of some organizational function or process.

There are only two brain regions that enable us to conceptualize the possible origin and regulatory control of our mental experiences: the *limbic system* as a driving source of our mental experiences and the *prefrontal cortex* as their regulatory agent.

THE LIMBIC SYSTEM

The suggestion that the limbic system is instrumental in the actualization of mental representations is based on its putative role in the phenomenon of dreaming as postulated below. Dreaming is experiencing activated internal images *while the RAS is turned off, as are, consequently, our memory banks.* How and where do these nightly activations originate while the brain is "asleep," as indicated by the slow wave pattern on the electroencephalogram? Why do they occur in four predictable REM stages?

The human limbic system is centrally positioned between the left and right hemispheres. It comprises the hypothalamus, hippocampi, parahippocampi, the cingulate and dentate gyri, septal region, and amygdaloid nuclei (see fig. 7). Except for the cingulate, hippocampal, and parahippocampal gyri, the limbic structures are, as the phylogenetically oldest structures of the brain, not part of the cerebral cortex and therefore not subject to the wakeup calls of the RAS. Their activities are *self-generated in individually specific circadian rhythms*, securing the provision of vital biological services around the clock.

Examples of these rhythmic activities are the twenty-four-hour

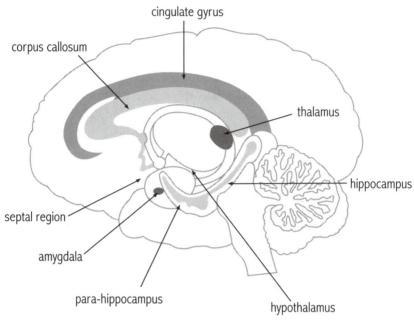

Fig. 7. The limbic system

fluctuations in the release of hormones produced by the hypothalamic centers, which regulate the pituitary release of prolactin, gonadotropins, testosterone, growth hormone, thyrotropin, and adrenocorticotropic hormone (ACTH). Because of the different release schedules, the plasma concentrations of each of these hormones show individually specific curves with differently timed peaks and bottoms throughout a twenty-four-hour period. The temporal consistency of the peaks and valleys during their nocturnal oscillations, the influence of peptides on dreaming,[2] and the consistent changes in REM sleep associated with reduced corticosteroid plasma levels in depressed individuals[3] suggest that these hormonal undulations are implicated in the occurrences of the four REM stages of dreaming in the absence of our mental capabilities.*

---

*Dreaming is often considered to be a mental experience. However, the dialectical differentiation between internal images and visual percepts required for our mental experiences cannot occur in the absence of actual visual percepts.

This postulate requires an explanation of the relationship between these hormonal activities and the activation of internal visual engrams. It has long been established that our emotional experiences originate in the subcallosal area of the limbic system referred to as the *septal region*. Its stimulation in animal studies results in a state of contentment and an increase in motor, social, and sexual activities; ablation results in complete apathy and total self-neglect. R. G. Heath successfully treated patients suffering from chronic depression by stimulating electrodes placed in the septal region.[4] The septal region is also affected positively or negatively by internal biochemical and hormonal changes as in postpartum depression, euphoric states induced by corticosteroid therapy, an abnormally functioning thyroid gland, or premenstrual conditions.

We may conclude, then, that the septal region is, even during sleep, periodically stimulated by the nightly fluctuations of diverse hormones. That these stimulations lead to the activation of visual engrams is a natural consequence of the mnemonic fusions that are formed between the septal region and the visual association cortex discussed below. *Their mnemonic reciprocity explains the periodic activations of internal images experienced as dreams as a consequence of the differently timed oscillations of various hormones during sleep.* This explanation is consistent with the fact that dreams are frequently accompanied by emotions.

Since hormonal undulations occur around the clock, we may assume that their visual engram activations continue during the daytime and even more frequently in light of the fact that various hormones peak more than once and some only during the day. Apart from these periodic activations during the waking states, the septal region in and by itself continually generates activities reflecting the circadian rhythms induced by the *suprachiasmatic nucleus* (SCN). These septal activities explain why normally functioning humans continually find themselves in a certain "frame of mind" during the day, hand in hand with motivational states and behavioral activities, and *the continual stream of our mental experiences, while the daily biochemical and hormonal fluctuations explain the surprise occurrences of a memory, a wish, or an enlightening "brainstorm" whose content is entirely unrelated to the content of ongoing mental activities.*

Since emotional experiences, like all other empirical mental events, cannot be mentally reproduced in and of themselves, how then can we speak of the existence of their *mnemonic* fusions with visual engrams? This problem is solvable by virtue of the *hippocampi*.

The hippocampi are horse-shaped structures embedded in the inferior medial temporal lobes (see fig. 7) yet considered to be part of the limbic system because of their neural connections with *every limbic area or nucleus*. It has long been known that the hippocampi have a major role in memory, motivation, and learning in humans as well as in lower species as far down as reptiles and chipmunks.[5] Bilateral ablation of the hippocampi in animals results in a complete loss of memory; lesions in both inferior temporal lobes in humans cause memory loss for recently perceived events. This memory loss is dramatic. R. M. Restak described the case of Clive, the world-renowned musician and musicologist with an encyclopedic knowledge of music, whose inferior temporal lobes were permanently destroyed by viral encephalitis. Restak reports: "He now spends his time sitting in a twelve-by-twelve hospital room playing endless games of solitaire and making entries in a notebook. The entries always are the same: Now I am awake, for the first time in years. Yet, he always disclaims having written these notes. Whenever his wife visits him he exuberantly greets her as if he has not seen her in years."[6]

An identical loss of the capacity to retain memories of new experiences or retrieve old ones was observed in twenty-seven-year-old H.M. following the neurosurgical removal of his medial temporal lobes (which contain the neural pathways that connect the hippocampi with the visual association cortex) to stop the spreading of his chronic epileptic condition.[7]

These clinical observations were preceded by the experimental investigations by H. Kluver.[8] Bilateral ablation of the temporal lobes in animals resulted in the "Kluver-Bucy" syndrome: compulsive oral intake but failure to recognize edible objects (as eating rocks), hypersexuality and with different species (a cat mounting a chicken), and lack of defensive activity upon provocation. The numerous subsequent laboratory investigations have confirmed that the hippocampi are indispensable for the establishment of memory in all species. Yet the actual process underlying this role has thus far remained unknown.

We should note, however, that past explicatory efforts focused on the hippocampi's role in the function of "remembering." To attribute such a role to the hippocampi conflicts with the dual concept of memory as conceived in part 1, which suggests that the sense of remembering is an *empirical* event that requires mnemonic content that is determined by the *gestalts* of visual engrams. The absence of a retinotopic or tonotopic cell structure in the hippocampi rules out the possibility that the hippocampi serves as storage centers for "long-term" memory, as is frequently suggested. This objection also applies to past suggestions that hypothalamic centers, the septal region, and the amygdaloid nuclei retain memories.[9]

Thanks to Mishkin's career-long research with monkeys, we now are aware of the existence of the *inferior longitudinal fasciculus*, which bundles the neural fibers that connect the hippocampi with the visual association cortex. These connections with the only conceivable storage centers of mnemonic content, and the fact that these fibers are reciprocal in impulse conductivity and the hippocampi also are neurally connected with other limbic centers and nuclei suggest that the hippocampi function as *relay stations of the mnemonic fusions formed between cognitive content and the entire gamut of emotional "memories."*

This notion of the hippocampi as "mediators"[10] (a term used by M. B. Arnold), combined with the concept of the cerebral/empirical foundation of our cognitive capacity, explains the complete loss of memory following destruction of the hippocampi as follows: Without the stimulation by the septal region and the consequent deprivation of activating our visual memory banks, it is impossible to experience the dialectical differences between internal images and actual visual percepts as required for the empirical notion of having experienced before.

Furthermore, the intact hippocampi's relay function makes it possible to conceptualize how we experience the "memories" of our limbic experiences in spite of the absence of mnemonic storage facilities. The hippocampal interruption divides the neural foundation of our mnemonic fusions between the visual memory banks and the limbic system into two neural pathways: (1) the aforementioned inferior longitudinal fasciculus, which connects the hippocampi with the visual memory banks, on the one hand, and (2) the neural fibers that connect the hippocampi with limbic areas, on the other hand.

This division reflects careful biological planning. We form mnemonic connections not only between the limbic system and the visual association cortex but with the auditory memory banks as well. Since the entire limbic area is considerably smaller than the visual and auditory association regions (the amygdaloid nuclei, for example, do not exceed the size of a pea), it appears inconceivable that it could accommodate the innumerable neural fibers connecting with all visual and auditory engrams if they were formed as straight neural pathways, that is, without the interruption of the hippocampi. The hippocampi are considerably larger than any limbic structure, and the fact that they are part of the neocortex (the inferior temporal lobe) and thus consist of six layers with innumerable dendrites,[11] which indicates that they have the capability to absorb all neural connections with our two memory banks. In contrast, the required number of hippocampal connections with the limbic areas is limited to only a few small areas: the pain and pleasure centers in the hypothalamus, the septal region as the origin of our emotions, and the amygdaloid nuclei (the vigilantes for self-preservation). This allows us to consider the possibility that the hippocampi form singular connections with *each given emotional quality of a given limbic center* but are capable of connecting each quality with the fibers of a multitude of visual and auditory engrams representing past events experienced in association with the given emotional quality. Consequently, when an internal visual engram is actualized, it activates the hippocampi, which, in turn, activate a mnemonically fused emotional quality that, because of the simultaneous experience of a mental event, is experienced with a sense of having experienced before, while the gestalt of the mental event provides information about when and where the remembered sensation took place.

The above suggests that limbic memory is a combination of an *actual* emotional experience (albeit of low intensity) and an intellectual event. These double activation productions of the hippocampi explain the high concentration of the excitatory neurotransmitter glutamate in the hippocampal regions. Although little information is available about the exact role of the *parahippocampi* in limbic activities, it is conceivable that they also are involved in the mediation of memory in view of their connections with the lateral sulcus.

We may conclude, then, that the septal region is the "generator" of our independent mental experiences and their continual occurrence during the waking states. Since we have, as in dreams, no control over which engrams may be activated by the septal region (each given emotion is associated with many different visual or auditory engrams), we are potentially subject to a kaleidoscopic array of actualized internal images. Yet the normally functioning human being shows a remarkable cohesiveness between the contents of successive mental experiences, which, as mentioned earlier indicates the existence of some regulatory process. To explore the origin and nature of this control, we need to turn to the prefrontal cortex.

THE PREFRONTAL CORTEX

The prefrontal cortex is the most anterior cortical portion of the frontal lobe. In contrast with most other cortical areas in the brain, its morphology and cytology are nonspecific, nor does it contain one specific neurotransmitter. In fact, all neurotransmitters found elsewhere in the brain are present in the prefrontal cortex, although there is a preponderance of GABA (gamma-aminobutyric acid), an inhibitory neurotransmitter.

Anatomically, it is a junction where neural pathways converge from every other brain area that retains memory of some kind: the visual and auditory association areas, the limbic system, the premotor cortex, and Broca's speech center. (The last two regions are situated in the dorsal portions of the frontal lobe adjacent to the prefrontal cortex and contain the neuronal blueprints of movements and speech.)

Although the prefrontal cortex has long been considered to be "the seat of intelligence," its actual function has yet to be established. Experimental electrical stimulation in animals has failed to elicit any specific result. Its function, or the consequences thereof, becomes apparent only by default, that is, by the emergence of clinical symptoms following lesions in the prefrontal cortex, such as tumors, or general paresis caused by spirochetal infection. The nature of these symptoms invariably reflect *intellectual deficits* in concentration, attention, and memory; *emotional erosion* (such as apathy, lack of rapport); and loss of *behavioral control* (bizarre conduct, lack of decorum). These symptoms do not form one specific syndrome, but make their appearance in unpredictable combinations of mental, emotional, and behavorial anomalies differing from patient to patient, so well described by M. M. Mesulam:

> Some of these patients become puerile, profane, slovenly, face-
> tious, irresponsible, grandiose and irascible; others lose spon-
> taneity, curiosity, initiative and develop apathetic blunting of
> feeling, drive, mentation and behavior; others show an erosion of
> foresight, judgment, insight and lose the ability to delay gratifica-
> tion and often the capacity for remorse; still others show an
> impairment of abstract reasoning, creativity, problem solving and
> mental flexibility, jump to premature conclusions and become
> excessively concrete or stimulus bound.[12]

Despite the large number of explorations conducted during the last three decades, the nature of the indisputable relationship between mental and behavioral activities and the prefrontal cortex still remains enigmatic. The only conspicuous certainty is the immense volume and complexity of neural pathways that connect the prefrontal cortex with other cortical areas and the limbic system in addition to an intricate internal neural circuitry as described in fine detail by Goldman-Rakic in 1987 and by J. M. Fuster in his volume *The Prefrontal Cortex* in 1989.[13]

Goldman-Rakic suggested that the "self-regulation" of mental, physical, and verbal activities could be conceived as the combined results of prefrontal neural circuitry and mental representational memory. But she also issued this caveat:

Unlike largely sensory and motor skills, the mnemonic, associative and command functions of the mammalian brain have eluded precise neurological explanation. The proposition that cognitive function(s) can be localized to specific neural circuits is not easy to defend because the neural interactions that underlie even the most simple concept or solution of an abstract problem have not been convincingly demonstrated. Also, it does not seem possible to conceptualize in neural terms what it means to generate an idea, to grasp the essentials of a situation, to be oriented in space and time, or to plan for long-range goals.[14]

Fuster concluded his manuscript as follows (italics by this author):

The prefrontal cortex supports several *cortical functions* (i.e., information processing functions) and that at least three of these functions can be identified as specific for that region of the neocortex: *provisional (short term) memory, preparatory set of motor actions, and interference control. Further, all three functions cooperate under a supraordinate function that is distinctive of the prefrontal cortex as a whole: the temporal organization of behavior.*[15]

Both Goldman-Rakic and Fuster advanced their theories at the end of the nineteenth century, when the nature and origin of mental experiences had yet to be clarified, which thus restricted the interpretations of their research. The proposed cerebral/empirical concept of the mind in part 1 extends their conclusions twofold. First, it meets Goldman-Rakic's caveat by providing a rationale of the dynamics of the mind and "its" mental experiences. Second, the clarification of the nature and origin of cognitive functions enables us to conceive a biological rationale for Fuster's notion of "interference control exercised by a supraordinate function."

However, we first need to note that the cerebral/empirical concept implies that the prefrontal cortex cannot be involved in cognitive functions such as information processing and provisional memory. Its lack of a specific cellular (for example, retinotopic or tonotopic) storage capacity excludes any capability of cognitive functions. Nor does it have any neural connections with the physical systems that receive and process auditory and visual sensory input. *Cognitive functions are the exclusive domains of the visual and auditory associative cortices because only their neuronal architecture permits the storage of cognitive content,* as detailed in chapters 7 and 9. These objections also apply to the notion of "a preparatory set of motor actions." As detailed in chapter 18, our memories of learned movements are, as in all primates, retained in the supplementary motor cortex as "behavioral templates."

It further is important to emphasize the fact that the abnormalities in mental, physical, and verbal activities observed during pathological changes in the prefrontal cortex do not reflect abnormalities in *functions* per se but indicate defects in the *appropriateness of their utilization* with regard to desirability, necessity, reality, or social norms.

An opportunity to conceptualize the process by which we control the appropriate employment of our mental and behavioral activities arises when we analyze the interesting phenomenon of "forgetting." As described in the first section of this chapter, we normally experience during the waking states a *continuous and irresistible* flow of memories, ideas, plans, and wishes, all reflecting mental contents determined by cerebral gestalts, and all accompanied by our experience of the dialectical, that is, empirical triad of self, nonself, and cognition. The irresistibility and continuity of our mental experiences during the waking states are the consequences of our diurnally lit-up memory banks by virtue of the reticular activating system.

Another source of actualizing mental experiences are such limbic activities as emotional or somatoceptive experiences, which originate in the septal region, hypothalamus, or amygdala. Their positive or negative qualities are stored in the parahippocampal pain and pleasure centers, where they are mnemonically fused via the hippocampus (the major seat of our mnemonic fusions) with simultaneously experienced visual or auditory percepts that are engrammed in the associative parietal cortices. Thus, when recurring emotions or somatoceptive sensations activate pleasurable or displeasurable memories, their activations are neurally relayed from the parahippocampus to the hippocampus, which, in turn, relays the stimulation to the mnemonically fused visual or auditory engrams. *Consequently, we are, in great measure, at the mercy of our limbic system with regard to the content of our intellectual experiences and the nature of their underlying emotional experiences.*

Because mental representations are the irresistible products of our constantly activated memory banks and our equally autonomously operating limbic system, we are not capable of *mentally suppressing our thoughts or memories or their mnemonically fused emotional qualities* in case these happen to be disagreeable or painful. However, most humans experience occasions when they are unable to mnemonically retrieve someone's name or telephone number, later realizing that this temporary "mental blockade" appeared to be related to some unpleasant emotional quality associated with the memory. Psychiatrists often observe a lasting amnesia (or "repression") of severely shameful or painful experiences, as exemplified in chapter 20.

This common experience of "forgetting" led Freud to conceive in 1895 what was then considered his most important contribution to psychology and psychiatry: the unconscious mind. However, this concept still has to be clarified (see chap. 11). The cerebral/empirical concept suggests that "unconscious" interference with our mental experiences can be attributed only to some *biological* system that, because it involves emotions, is likely to be part of our limbic system. There exists, indeed, a set of limbic components that possess the capacity of "turning off" disagreeable cerebral activities, namely: the amygdaloid nuclei.

THE AMYGDALOID NUCLEI

The "amygdalae" are situated in the anterior pole of the left and right temporal cortices (see fig. 7). Only the size of a pea, they consist of three clusters of nuclei: a *corticomedial* group, a *basolateral* group, and the *central* nucleus, each of which is neurally connected with the limbic and olfactory system, the thalamus, hypothalamus, the RAS, and the autonomous nervous system (ANS), which all have an essential role in that unique, innate function of the amygdalae:

self-preservation. For example, experimental stimulation of the amygdalae provokes in all animals endowed with a central nervous system actions to fight or flee, or freeze ("play dead," as opossums do), or change skin color (by chameleons). Peaceful monkeys become ferociously aggressive; other species engage in feeding-like actions (licking, sniffing, swallowing, or retching), while cats hiss and claw with fur standing up.

On the other hand, bilateral ablation of the *anterior temporal lobes* results in the "Kluver-Bucy" syndrome: compulsive oral intake without differentiating between edible and nonedible objects (such as eating rocks), hypersexuality but with inappropriate species (a cat mounting a chicken), defensive actions absent when provoked, and impaired memory because of the involvement of the hippocampus. Similar changes without memory loss but including profound alterations in *approach and avoidance behavior* also occur following bilateral *amygdalectomy*. Any combination of the deviations described above may occur in humans who are afflicted by prefrontal disease.

The combined results of the laboratory experiments and clinical observations described above allow the following interpretations:

1. The occurrence of the "prefrontal syndrome" following pathological changes in the prefrontal cortex indicates that the prefrontal cortex has an indispensable role in the effective utilization of our mental, physical, and verbal activities.
2. Amygdalectomy also causes the occurrence of a prefrontal syndrome, which indicates that the functionality of the prefrontal cortex is under control of the amygdalae.
3. Since the prefrontal cortex has never been shown to produce any specific mental, behavioral, or verbal function, its functionality can be attributed only to the neural pathways, suggesting the probability that the amygdalae exert their influence by altering neural conductivity in the prefrontal circuits.
4. The latter suggestion is not only consistent with the large number of neural pathways in the prefrontal cortex, it becomes most evident when we mentally "dissect" the functionality of these neural pathways by applying the oberva-

tions of Goldman-Rakic and Fuster. We then become aware of the identical functions of three neural circuits, each of which connects the prefrontal cortex with another cortical area. One circuit uses the *superior, longitudinal fasciculus* (see fig. 8) to connect the prefrontal cortex with the *visual and auditory associative cortices* in the parietal lobes; another pathway connects it with the *premotor cortex*; the third one connects *Broca's speech center* with the prefrontal cortex. These three cortical regions are the very cerebral areas where our intellectual, behavioral, and verbal activities originate. All three neural circuits are reciprocal.

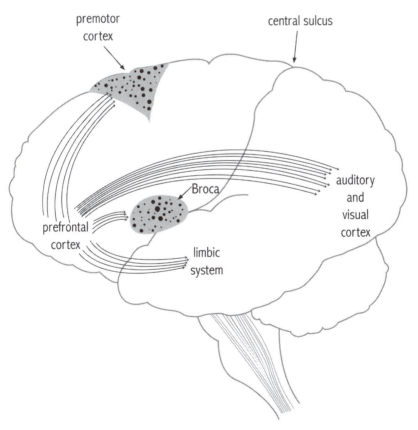

Fig. 8. Prefrontal cortex connections

To illustrate how the frontally situated amygdalae censor the neural activity of undesirable mental representations located way back in the posterior brain, I employ the previously mentioned phenomenon of "mental repression." When we experience a thought, memory, or particular wish that is associated with an intolerable, embarrassing, or frigthening emotion, such feeling is aroused whenever its mnemonically fused visual engram is actualized. This activation is relayed via the hippocampus to the parahippocampus, which then "alerts" the amygdalae, which then, via their neural connection with the prefrontal cortex, induce the deactivation of the activated cellular representation in the prefrontal cortex of the mental representation that initiated the event. This blockade can be conceived as follows.

The *central region* of the prefrontal cortex where the amygdaloid fibers end is composed of *granular cells*. Granular cells are cortical neurons that are multipolar interneurons with branched dendrites and a short axon that arborizes and synapses with other cortical neurons in the immediate vicinity, such as stellate cells. Stellate cells are local circuit neurons that compose two functionally different groups, namely, excitatory and inhibitory neurons, which have the capacity of either excreting neuroexcitatory neurotransmitters or inhibitory ones like GABA.[16] These excretions are *autonomous* biological events whose stimulations and inhibitions control, for example, the cerebellum's function of maintaining our postural equilibrium. In the absence of any other explanation, we may conceive then that the GABA neurotransmitters inactivate the "lit-up" fibers that reciprocally relay the inihibition to the actualized visual engram in the parietal cortex via the superior longitudinal fasciculus, as discussed above. The same scenario can be applied to the other two neural (motor and verbal) circuits to explain how we refrain from inappropriate statements or actions while we are speaking or engaged in social interactions.

The anatomical, neurophysiological, and functional similarities between the three prefrontal circuits whose inhibitory actions are exclusively censored by the amygdaloid nuclei indicate that the inhibitory control by the prefrontal cortex is an innate function in all species that possess a central nervous system. While the amygdalae in infrahuman species serve to protect the animal's physical existence, in humans they mainly utilize the prefrontal cortex to preserve internal psychological harmony, intellectual efficiency, and social integrity.

NOTES

1. M. Bunge, *The Mind-Body Problem* (Oxford: Pergamon Press, 1980).

2. J. A. Hobson, *The Dreaming Brain* (New York: Basic Books, 1977).

3. E. J. Sachar et al., "Cortisol Production in Depressive Illness," *Archives of General Psychiatry* 23, no. 4 (1970): 289–98.

4. R. M. Restak, *The Brain* (Garden City, NY: Doubleday, 1979).

5. R. L. Isaacson, *The Limbic System* (New York: Plenum Press, 1982).

6. R. M. Restak, *The Mind* (New York: Bantam Books, 1988).

7. E. F. Loftus and G. R. Loftus, "On the Permanence of Stored Information in the Human Brain," *American Psychologist* 35, no. 5 (May 1980): 409–20.

8. H. Kluver and P. C. Bucy, "Kluver-Bucy Syndrome," *Biological Psychiatry* 10: 65–68.

9. C. R. Noback, N. L. Strominger, and R. J. Demarest, *The Human Nervous System*, 4th ed. (Philadelphia: Lea & Febiger, 1991).

10. M. B. Arnold, *Memory and the Brain* (Hillsdale, NJ: Lawrence Erlbaum Associates, 1984).

11. G. Lynch, *Synapses, Circuits, and the Beginning of Memory* (Cambridge, MA: MIT Press, 1986).

12. M. M. Mesulam, "Frontal Cortex and Behavior," *Annals of Neurology* 19 (1986): 320–25.

13. P. Goldman-Rakic, "Circuitry of the Prefrontal Cortex: Short-Term Memory and the Regulation of Behavior by Representational Knowledge," *Handbook of Physiology: Higher Functions of the Nervous System* (Bethesda, MD: American Physiological Society, 1987); J. M. Fuster, *The Prefrontal Cortex: Anatomy, Physiology and Neuropsychology of the Frontal Lobe*, 2nd ed. (New York: Raven Press, 1989).

14. Goldman-Rakic, "Circuitry of the Prefrontal Cortex."

15. Fuster, *Prefrontal Cortex*.

16. Noback, Strominger, and Demarest, *The Human Nervous System*.

PART 3
STRUCTURES OF THE MIND

11

EGO, SUPEREGO, ID

The first suggestion of mental structures appeared in 1895 in Freud's essay "Psychology for Neurologists" (a title his editors changed to "Project for a Scientific Psychology"). In this essay, Freud tentatively divided the mind into three "layers": the conscious, preconscious, and unconscious. In 1923 he replaced this "topographic" concept with his "psychodynamic" model, whose structures he described with the now-immortal terms *ego*, *superego*, and *id*.

Consistent with his belief that the mind is a product of the brain, he continued to emphasize that these hypothetical structures would also be proven to be cerebral in origin. At this time of writing, that is, three-quarters of a century later, this prophecy has yet to be fulfilled. Only few attempts have been undertaken. In 1966, J. Eccles suggested that the two most prominent ego functions (the sense of self and consciousness) originate in the dominant cerebral hemisphere.[1] In 1989, L. Tinnen also suggested, in his article "The Anatomy of the Ego," that the left brain is the neural substrate of the ego.[2] But neither publication addressed the quintessential issue of how neuronal activities in a specific brain region convert into mental experiences.

While Freud's concepts of the ego, superego, and id have become the cornerstones of all theories on psychological development and psychological functioning, we still entered the new millennium without any idea about the nature of these mental structures or whether they actually exist.

The persistence of this explanatory hiatus brings to mind a statement Freud once made in regard to his structural concept of the mind: "It is entirely possible that future advances in our biological understanding of the brain may completely obliterate the validity of these hypothetical structures."

Such obliteration is the very consequence when we apply the cerebral/empirical model of the mind that reflects the recent discoveries in the neurophysiology of the brain. As detailed in chapter 4, this model defines the mind as a conceptual conglomerate of innumerable mental representations, each of which consists of two components: a *cerebral* component (an activated visual or auditory engram) and a *nonphysical* (mental) component, namely, the sense of knowing or having experienced before. This sense of cognition was conceived in chapter 4 to emerge as an empirical epiphenomenon by virtue of our simultaneous experiences of the dialectical differences between extraneously originating actual visual or auditory percepts versus internally activated images or auditory memories. This view that our mental experiences are empirical, that is, strictly experiential epiphenomena, implies that Freud's concept of the permanent existence of mental structures, each empowered with specific mental functions, is not a tenable prospect.

The only conceivable mental structures are our mental representations, of which the visual ones are the most prominent. Visual mental representations originate as activated visual engrams (see chap. 7) whose neuronal configurations not only are the sole determinants of the cognitive contents of all our mental activities, the consistency of these contents, their dullness, and retrievability—as opposed to the sharpness and ever-changing content of actual visual percepts—cause us to experience activated visual engrams with a sense of having experienced before and thus as mental representations. Furthermore, the neuronal foundation of our mental representations and their imperative role in our dialectical realization of mental epiphenomena confirm Freud's prediction that all mental experiences would be proven to originate as cerebral activities.

The psychological involvement of cerebral activities is further apparent from the *autonomous* formations of *mnemonic fusions* between visual engrams and other brain areas by means of neural pathways, as described in chapter 6. These reciprocal interneuronal connections explain why we experience our mental events with a specific and usually lasting subjective meaning and how a given feeling state may actuate a certain mental state.

All of the above also applies to the neuronal representations of our auditory and linguistic experiences (see chap. 9), including their formation of mnemonic fusions with visual engrams. These triple neuronal interconnections explain our ability to mentally retrieve previously experienced empirical qualities (such as our sense of cognition or consciousness) or sensorial events (such as pain or happiness), which cannot be remembered in and by themselves.

In view of the unlikely existence of the traditional mental structures as concluded above, the question arises whether the terms *ego*, *superego*, and *id* are still useful. An answer emerges when we compare the mental *functions* that Freud attributed to the ego, superego, and id with the mental *consequences* of our mental representations according to the cerebral/empirical concept.

THE EGO

Freud conceived "the" ego as a mental agency whose functions include our sense of self and consciousness, our perceptions of the external world, the formation and storage of memory, behavioral control, and the development and utilization of psychological defense mechanisms to cope with our internal psychological conflicts. These formulations were the beginning of what is presently known as ego psychology, whose contemporary proponents have redefined the functions of the ego in four categories: the regulation of instinctual drives, object (i.e., interpersonal) relations, the relation to reality, and primary autonomous functions.[3]

According to the cerebral/empirical model, most of these psychological events are not *mental functions*. Perceptions are not mental events but naturally and autonomously occurring cerebral experiences. Only our perceptual *interpretations* are mental events that involve the mnemonic use of our previous perceptual experiences and their mnemonically fused emotional and somatoceptive memories. Neither is memory a specific cerebral or mental function but, as illustrated in chapter 1, an empirical epiphenomenon that occurs only when we simultaneously experience the gestalts of actualized internal images and the dialectically opposing gestalts of actual visual percepts.

Furthermore, mental "functions," such as thinking, planning, and reminiscing, are not functions of some mental agency but different modes of employing visual mental representations induced and guided by our emotional and somatoceptive states, as detailed in chapter 10.*

Finally, our sense of self and of consciousness are not functions of some hypothetical mental structure but are empirical epiphenomena (see chap. 3). The experiences of these qualities are associated with the empirical quality of cognition. Because we cannot realize our sense of selfness as such without realizing our sense of cognition as such, and because our sense of cognition would not occur without the differentiation between the selfness of our internal images and the nonselfness of visual percepts, I suggested in chapter 3 that these inextricable experiences form a dialectical *self/nonself/cognition triad*. This triad thus serves as the foundation of our inextricable awareness of self and consciousness.

Even though our sense of selfness is an empirical event and thus cannot in and of itself attain the status of permanence, we usually experience a notion of "our self" as an absolute entity. This notion can be explained when we explore a statement repeatedly emphasized by Freud, that is, "the Ego is first and foremost a Body Ego," although he never offered a clarification of the process(es) involved.

As detailed in chapter 13, our concept of the *bodily self* (or body ego) reflects our realization of the body as our exclusive self *object*,

---

*All of the above resonates with Rosenfield's arguments in his book *The Invention of Memory* questioning the general notion of the existence of mental functions.[4]

as the *sole source* of our somatoceptive sensations, and the *vehicle* that only we can move about. Since the body is a material object and thus permanently present in our visual field, *we constantly perceive and recognize, visually and somatoceptively, its qualities of selfness as a permanent characteristic of the body.*

We visually perceive our body as we perceive any other visible object, that is, we form of every body percept a visual engram that, when internally activated, is experienced as a body image. Even though we usually perceive the body as an intact object, because of the many different postures we ordinarily assume and the many different activities and movements we perform with different body parts, we also form a considerable number of "partial" body images. Since we constantly perceive our body in our visual field, we incessantly recognize during the waking states the ever-presence of our body, hand in hand with our recognitions of our continuous somatoceptive experiences. Thanks to the ingeniously engineered mnemonic fusions between cerebral engrams and the motor centers in the brain (see chap. 18), we automatically and naturally initiate and control our bodily movements and so experience our body as a material self-object. This notion is constantly reinforced by means of (1) the mnemonic fusions formed between somatoceptive motoric experiences and body images and (2) the dialectical realization of the nonselfness of the bodily existence of others.

While all body images naturally are integral components of the conceptual conglomerate of mental representations that we experience as "the mind," their underlying visual engrams are, like all other visual engrams, stored in the visual association cortex in the order of their chronological occurrence (see chap. 3) so that there is not one cohesive engram that represents the entire body. However, because our body images are constantly activated during the waking states, we mentally experience them as components of one body concept.

Consequently, we form, or rather experience, two different self-concepts: one concept composed of body images mentally unified in the *bodily self* and one concept comprising non–bodily related mental representations, which all are mnemonically fused with intellectual and emotional memories and thus unified into the mental, that is, *psychological self.*

Because both forms involve the experience of the self/non-self/cognition triad, it is questionable that "the" ego is first and foremost a body ego. The empirical nature of this triad also is inconsistent with Freud's notion that the ego is a division of the mind and endowed with mental functions such as sense of selfness and consciousness, perception and storage of memory, and so on.

Because all visual engrams are stored in our visual memory banks, these storage banks thus are the cerebral foundations of the mind. They serve as our internal, ever-accessible library of our memories of all past experiences and their mnemonic fusions with our emotional and somatoceptive memories, thus creating our internal universe of our accomplishments, failures, desires, emotional needs, hopes, plans, anticipations, and relationships with friends and loved ones, all of this contained in individual visual mental representations that we collectively call the mind. Despite the scattered location of their underlying visual engrams in the visual association cortex, certain engrams have a certain quality in common, which leads by means of their mnemonic fusions with specific linguistic engrams to a conceptual mental entity such as the bodily self and the superego.

THE SUPEREGO

Freud conceived the superego as a mental agency, a childhood product formed as the result of the child's identification with the beliefs and values of the parents and other authority figures. He postulated that the superego consists of two subsystems: the conscience, which punishes the person for noncompliance with rules and expectations, and the ego ideal, which represents the child's notion that compliant actions will earn him or her parental reward and thus promote self-pride. Both systems are presumed to be responsible for three main functions: the control of sexual and aggressive impulses, the pursuit of moralistic goals, and the urge for perfection.

While Freud's concept of the ego was universally accepted in its original version, his concept of the superego has continually been subject to different interpretations and reformulations.[5] These differences mainly revolve around the origin of the superego and the chronology of its development described by Normund Wong in his inclusive overview in volume 1 of the 1989 edition of the *Comprehensive Textbook of Psychiatry.*

Wong's overview also indicates that all versions agree with Freud's notions that the superego is an independent psychic structure within the psychic apparatus, largely unconscious, the product of the child's identification with the beliefs of parents and authority figures, and the singular source of guilt. However, such crucial questions as what process precipitates guilt, or how to conceive the superego as a *"partially" unconscious mental operation,* are not addressed.

The majority of superego theories are based on clinical observations of guilt or shame experienced in psychopathological conditions such as neuroses, psychoses, or personality disorders. The following exploration of what may constitute the superego and the nature of its role in the development of guilt and shame takes a different approach by focusing on the processes by which the beliefs, attitudes, and moral principles are carried over to the child during his or her everyday interactions with parents, teachers, siblings, and peers.

The term *identification* is not used in this effort because it is not clearly defined and as used by Freud ("identification is like becoming someone else") does not offer a natural explanation of the formation of the superego and its two systems of conscience and ego ideal. I believe that R. Schafer's concept of internalization[6] offers the most realistic description of how humans at all ages internalize and retain the thoughts, views, and beliefs of others. Furthermore, because there would be no guilt or shame without some kind of action or appearance, our discussion also underscores the indispensable role of human physical and verbal activities.

From the most rudimentary beginnings of his linguistic input, the child's actions and behaviors are continually subject to environmental appraisals, encouragements, and prohibitions. The resulting auditory engrams of appraisals and the *visual engrams of appraisers* are simultaneously internalized and mnemonically fused with the *behavioral templates that underlie the child's appraised behaviors*, the body images which he eventually forms of his bodily activities (detailed in part 4), and the *emotional and somatoceptive memories* of the feelings evoked by the environmental appraisals, such as the satisfying sensation of accomplishment experienced following a warm compliment for the child "being so nice" to a sibling or the feeling of embarrassment, shame, or guilt caused by harsh criticism or belittling statements.

The mnemonic fusions between these simultaneous experiences result in the formation of complex "biological," that is, *neuronal modules*, which, when activated, result in distinct mnemonic experiences, each consisting of a combination of a *body image* (reflecting a given behavior); an *auditory engram* (external verbal appraisal); an *extraneous body image* (reflecting the nonverbal reactions by the appraiser), a *global gestalt*, which reflects the environmental setting in which the original perceptions occurred; and the mnemonically fused *emotional or somatoceptive* memories formed during the original experiences.

These mnemonic modules become the child's psychological instruments with which he or she eventually reviews how his or her attitudes, demeanor, and verbalized opinions and beliefs were, and thus will be, judged and reacted to by others.

As is the case with all other forms of memories, we are not capable of forming or reproducing the various mnemonic modules all at once. However, they all have the same specific feature of environmental approval and disapproval of our conduct in common. This commonality leads us to conceptually unify these mnemonic modules into a mental entity comparable to our formation of the body ego by means of our body images. Because this extraneous body images entity serves as a self-protective "rule book" for what is appropriate and acceptable in interpersonal and social interactions and what the adverse consequences may be in case of noncompliance, I believe that Freud's term *superego* is an appropriate description of this mental entity.

This view is thus different from the traditional psychoanalytic view of the superego as an independent agency that presumably is in constant intrapsychic battle with the ego to maintain moral standards and to control the id's unacceptable sexual and aggressive drives, while its subsystem, the conscience, serves as the executor to punish the person for noncompliance with rules and expectations.

This alleged punitive role of the conscience leads us to another difference with the "interpersonal" superego as conceived above, namely, compliance with the superego's rules is by no means a matter of automatic obedience to one's conscience. For instance, an individual will carefully control the effects of his or her actions on the feelings and opinions of loved ones and friends or individuals who are in a position of authority yet may ignore the feelings and opinions of people who are personally, socially, or professionally of no significance to him or her. Or an individual may feel pressed to expiate a regrettable deed in one personal relationship but shows no remorse in another. Even individuals with obsessive-compulsive character traits, who are traditionally considered to be suffering from an unusually harsh superego that presumably forces scrupulous adherence to certain principles or rituals, may show a surprising indifference to the feelings or opinions of nonsignificant others or a paradoxical sloppiness despite the preoccupation with perfection. It can be argued, then, that an individual's compliance with his or her superego is negotiable depending on the particular nature of interpersonal or social relationships and the individual's conscience, which can be conceived as multifaceted part of personality makeup (see chap. 19) rather than the executor of a castigatory superego.

The above suggests that feelings of shame, guilt, and remorse are not "automatic" products of a fixed mental agency but related to one's interpersonal relationships and one's personality makeup, which is a product of human interactions and relationships. Individuals who care about their social reputation, friendships, family ties, or marital relationship feel saddened or ashamed when letting down friends or loved ones if their actions may have caused a particularly meaningful person to experience emotional pain or left the impression that the other person is not loved or respected. Guilt, shame, and remorse naturally evolve from human relationships because all these are dialectical in nature (see chap. 17).

Lack of self-reproach reflects psychopathology when, for instance, an individual is not or does not wish to be involved with others, as so well described in H. Cleckley's work *The Mask of Sanity.*[7] Internally originating delusions of guilt as observed in depressions reflect specific psychodynamics discussed in part 5. Inability to retain or adhere to societal rules may reflect cerebral pathology, such as a malfunctioning prefrontal cortex, as discussed in the section on psychopathology.

In summary, according to the cerebral/empirical model of the mind, the superego is not a mental agency in charge of specific functions but a mnemonic entity whose mnemonic modules constantly remind us (by means of mnemonic fusions) of environmental reactions to and judgments of our behavioral and verbal activities and conduct. Compliance with its rules is a function of our conscience in human relationships, while legal and other authoritarian regulations are dealt with intellectually.

THE ID

Had Freud been aware of the functions of the limbic system as we presently know them, he might not have included the id as a mental entity. He used the term *id* (Latin for "it") to refer to a mental structure that he conceived to be the source of human's drives and instincts and the answer to the ultimate question that every theoretician or practitioner in psychology and psychiatry must face: What propels our mental experiences?

Freud adopted the term in 1923 from G. Groddeck (an internist specialized in psychosomatic medicine) and assigned it as the primordial reservoir of "psychic energy" by assuming that ideas, wishes, and impulses are infused with energy by the binding of instinctual drives to internalized "objects." He denominated this energy infusion as "cathexis." While the above processes have remained fundamental to psychoanalytical theory and its derivative branches, their factuality has never been substantiated. The now firmly established functions of the limbic system[8] enable us to identify the origin and nature of all functions attributed to the id, with the exception of the concept of the "unconscious."

The anatomical foundation of the id had already been discovered in 1887 by Broca, but its functional significance did not become apparent before 1933 (ten years after Freud published his structural concept of the mind), when Papez reported the existence of an organized circuitry between the different limbic structures. Since then numerous studies with both animals and human subjects have identified distinct functions in distinct limbic areas of which I highlight the following four cerebral sections, which are pertinent to our current discussion.

The septal (subcallosal) region. Stimulation of the septal region results in grooming behavior, a state of contentment and sexual arousal; ablation leads to self-neglect, motor inactivity, and social and sexual indifference.

Amygdaloid nuclei. Stimulation of the lateral segments of these pea-sized nuclei results in an "angry" animal easily provoked to attack. When the medial portion is stimulated, an animal will show anger or fear when threatened, but it does not initiate defensive actions. This indicates the self-preserving role of the amygdaloids in response to external threats. Idiopathic activities of these nuclei in humans are the cause of "periodic violence."[9]

The hypothalamus. The primary function of the hypothalamus is to maintain biological homeostasis, which is accomplished by a diversity of autochthonous physiological and endocrine regulatory actions that, thus, also serve the function of self-preservation. Stimulation of its anterior and lateral portions results in irritability and aggressiveness; excitation of the medial portion causes placidity; stimulation of the posterior section results in fearful states comparable to human states of anxiety (increased heart rate and blood pressure, diaphoresis, and pupillary dilatation). J. Olds and P. Milner and R. G. Heath and W. A. Mickle uncovered the existence of "pleasure centers"; J. M. R. Delgado discovered an "aversion or punishment" center, but it is possible that some of these findings are reflections of mnemonic fusions between the hypothalamus and other limbic areas.[10]

The suprachiasmatic nucleus. Because the functions of the different limbic structures are autochthonous occurrences in twenty-four-hour circadian rhythms controlled by the suprachiasmatic nucleus, which is stituated in the anterior portion of the hypothalamus, they explain the daily, time-related feeding activities in animals and their periodic mating activities. They also explain why we continually experience thoughts, memories, and such, thanks to the actualization of visual mental representations during the waking states and the experience of dreams during sleep (see chap. 10). *The limbic system thus is the source of psychic energy, our drives, our impulses, and our motivations.*

In addition to our irrepressibly occurring mental experiences, we are also capable of selectively actualizing visual mental representations for the purpose of reviewing past experiences and projecting the consequences of future activities. Because all these memories, ideas, and thoughts are mnemonically fused with emotional or somatoceptive memories, most mental activities are associated with feeling states, some pleasurable, some displeasurable, and some even outright frightening and causing anxiety. Since all limbic activities occur autonomously, no emotional or somatoceptive memory can be *mentally* repressed. Under these circumstances, another (just mentioned) function of the limbic system comes into action: the elimination of the provoking thought by blocking its underlying visual engram by the amygdaloid nuclei in concert with the prefrontal cortex, as described in the section on the prefrontal cortex in chapter 10. Being unfamiliar with these functions of the limbic system or the prefrontal cortex, Freud believed that repression rendered memories unconscious and subsequently stored in the id, which he conceived as the seat of "the unconscious," another hallmark of psychoanalytic theory yet to be clarified.

THE UNCONSCIOUS

It has occasionally been questioned: Is the unconscious necessary? More fundamental is the question: Does it exist?

It is an irrefutable fact that many humans carry along in their visual memory banks various "dormant" visual engrams unknown to themselves until their existence becomes apparent during psycho-analysis or psychotherapy, which then also reveals how such hidden memories affected an individual's emotional and intellectual states or behaviors despite their dormant status. As indicated by the two questions above, the persisting problem is whether these conditions are properly explained by Freud's concepts of the unconscious.

It is generally held that Freud's greatest contribution to science was the development of his concept of "the unconscious mind."[11] This concept emerged after his discovery of the existence of *repressed* ideas, wishes, or painful memories as manifest in dreams and described in his monumental work *The Interpretations of Dreams*.

This discovery led to Freud's concept of topographic layers of the mind and the conscious, preconscious, and unconscious. When he later replaced this concept with the ego, superego, and id model, he conceived the id as a "holding station" for repressed (i.e., "uncon-scious") memories, ideas, and wishes presumably deposited by the superego in this "unconscious structure" of the mind. This idea prompts several comments based on our current knowledge, which was unavailable to Freud.

First, if the cerebral/empirical model of the mind is a tenable propo-sition, then there can be no "unconscious mind" because all mental events are experienced with our sense of selfness and consciousness.

Second, the assumption that the limbic system serves as a depos-itory for improper sexual desires or painful or shameful memories is literally groundless because there are no areas in the limbic system that possess the required neuronal architecture for the mnemonic storage or "holding" of visual and auditory engrams. The only regions in the brain capable of forming and retaining visual and auditory engrams are the visual and auditory association cortices.

Third, not only is the notion that the superego is partially unconscious difficult to comprehend, it also is inexplicable how the superego could transfer engrams from our memory banks to the limbic system for storage after "turning them unconscious."

The cerebral/empirical theory of the mind suggests the following view of "unconscious" mental events based on naturally occurring events. All mnemonic experiences consist of two components: mnemonic content, which is determined by the cerebral gestalt of visual engrams, and the dialectical notion of "having perceived before." The "psychic energy" necessary for the activation of visual engrams originates in the limbic system (see chap. 10). The limbic system also contains the amygdaloid nuclei, which serve as a defense system in the service of self-preservation in all species in case of external, actual, or imminent danger. Because of our ability to mentally, that is, internally, review memories, we humans may also experience *internally arising anxiety or fear or imminent threat* when we experience memories that are mnemonically fused with unpleasant or frightening qualities. There is no conceivable reason to not expect that at such moments the amygdaloid nuclei will step in with their defensive means of fight, flight, or freeze.

Since such limbic events as emotions cannot be "repressed," the only available option is to repress the activation of the threatening memory, that is, to prevent the activation of its underlying visual engram. Accordingly, the amygdaloid nuclei induce via their neural pathways to the prefrontal cortex the inhibition of the bidirectional neural pathways between the prefrontal cortex and the visual memory bank and so subdues the troubling memory.

Because these neurophysiological processes are natural events that occur autonomously and irresistibly without the need for volitional actions, the *blocked actualization* of a given memory prevents the owner's awareness of its existence. Strictly speaking, this unawareness reflects the repression of the activation of a particular visual engram or engrams rather than the "making unconscious" of a mental representation by means of a mental "structure" such as the superego.

While visual engrams can be restrained from being activated by means of the amygdaloid nuclei and the prefrontal cortex, their mnemonically fused emotional or somatoceptive memories are, as mentioned, like all limbic events not suppressible. Since each given emotional or somatoceptive memory is mnemonically fused with numerous different visual engrams, there are ample opportunities for expression in acceptable (although not always practical) ways, which explains Freud's observation that "repressed memories continue to have a life on their own" and therefore affect intellectual or behavioral functions.

The above also applies to speech, as is evident, for example, when we meet a friend or acquaintance and immediately recognize him or her but cannot remember his or her name if such memory is associated with unpleasant feelings.

Our answers to the two questions cited at the opening of this section are, then: There is no conceivable cerebral or mental structure to accommodate the concept of "the" unconscious, nor is such structure necessary. While Freud viewed repression as a psychological defense mechanism, the above suggests that the inhibition of activating selected memories is a *natural function of the limbic system, thus a biological process.* Further aspects of biological and psychological defense mechanisms are discussed in chapter 19.

—•—

In summary, according to the cerebral/empirical interpretation of the mind, Freud was entirely correct when he warned that his hypothetically conceived mental structures ego, superego, and id could be obliterated by future enhancement of our biological knowledge of the brain. Still, his nomenclatural choices turn out to be serendipitous: The ego and superego exactly describe our concepts and experiences of the mental self and our behavioral principles toward others, while the "id/it" most appropriately describes the limbic system as the source of our invisible psychic energy.

NOTES

1. J. C. Eccles, *Brain and Conscious Experience* (Heidelberg: Springer, 1966).

2. L. Tinnen, "The Anatomy of the Ego," *Journal of Psychiatry* 52 (1989): 404–409.

3. Normund Wong, in *Comprehensive Textbook of Psychiatry*, 2 vols., ed. H. I. Kaplan and B. J. Sadock (Baltimore: Williams & Wilkins, 1989).

4. I. Rosenfield, *The Invention of Memory* (New York: Basic Books, 1988).

5. R. Blanck and G. Blanck, *Beyond Ego Psychology* (New York: Columbia University Press, 1986); R. Harre and R. Lamb, *The Encyclopedic Dictionary of Psychology* (Cambridge, MA: MIT Press, 1983).

6. R. Schafer, *Aspects of Internalization* (New York: International Universities Press, 1968).

7. H. Cleckley, *The Mask of Sanity* (St. Louis: Mosby, 1964).

8. S. Salloway, P. Malloy, and J. L. Cummings, *The Neuropsychiatry of Limbic and Subcortical Disorders* (Washington, DC: APA Press, 1997).

9. H. P. Pincus and G. J. Tucker, *Behavioral Neurology* (New York: Oxford University Press, 1985).

10. J. M. R. Delgado, *Physical Control of the Mind* (New York: Harper & Row, 1969).

11. E. Jones, *The Life and Work of Sigmund Freud*, part 1 (New York: Basic Books, 1953).

12

THE NEUROPHYSIOLOGY OF DREAMING

Dreaming is generally considered to be a mental activity, a notion that is incompatible with the cerebral/empirical concept of mental experiences. Yet it is briefly discussed here because of its supportive implications for the theoretical postulates presented thus far.

Dreaming is experiencing activated visual engrams that are, however, not actualized as mental representations because the absence of visual percepts prevents the experience of our dialectical sense of cognition.

The fact that dreaming occurs during sleep when the RAS is turned off, the entire cerebral cortex is resting, the visual memory banks are not lit up, exteroceptive input is halted at the reticular formation, and the self/nonself/cognition triad occurs only marginally if at all indicates that the activation of visual engrams during sleep is not dependent upon the mind. What, then, might be the origin of this activation?

E. Aserinsky and N. Kleitman serendipitously discovered that dreaming is associated with rapid eye movement (REM) activity and occurs in four twenty-minute periods alternating with seventy-minute periods of non-REM sleep.[1] McCarley and Hobson isolated in the brain stem (the seat of the RAS) two opposing but reciprocally interacting groups of neurons: cholinergic cells, which generate REM activity, and aminergic cells which inactivate REM-activity. They conceived these "REM-on cells" and "REM-off cells" as the *dream state generator*.[2]

But the process by which this generator is regulated so to produce REM states at four predictable intervals remains to be explained. Hobson conceived in 1988 the activation-synthesis hypothesis, which suggests that the content of dreams is synthesized by the forebrain, that is, the prefrontal cortex. However, such function of the prefrontal cortex has never been established, nor is there a need for the synthesis of dream content because it is the natural reflection of the gestalts of activated visual engrams.

The notion that dreaming is experiencing activated global visual engrams is supported by the following two observations.

1. *Dream activity ceases following lesions in the nondominant brain.* Patients who have undergone right hemispherectomy or suffered lesions in the right brain no longer dream.[3] This finding is consistent with the left/right lateralization of the mnemonic storage of linguistic versus global visual percepts, respectively (see chap. 8).

2. *The association of dreaming with REM activity.* Hobson's model assumes that REM activity is the cause of dreaming because the REM-activating cholinergic cells in the dream state generator fire about one second before the occurrence of REM activity. However, as indicated below, REM activity and actual dreaming are not necessarily synchronized. In fact, two arguments can be made that REM activity is not the cause but the consequence of dreaming. First, there is during sleep no conceivable purpose for the occurrence of ocular movements. During the waking states, they reflect our natural and irresistible occupation of scanning our global visual fields. We also scan our internally activated visual images, as is evident from the bursts of neuronal activity in the visual association cortex when an individual is asked to imagine visual memories during the waking state. Second, the unusual velocity of eye movements during dreaming can be explained by the fact that dreaming is not reexperiencing the original occurrence of pre-

vious visual events but experiencing activated visual engrams that are minute replicas of retinal images and closely filed together in the visual memory banks according to the sequence of perceptions. Consequently, a small area in the visual association cortex covers a large volume of visual memories so that, for example, an entire episode of a two-week vacation can be scanned and thus dreamed in a matter of minutes.

Besides the quest for the origin of engram activation during sleep, there is the question of why REM activity takes place in four predictable periods during one night of sleep. Both issues can be explained by way of the limbic system *because it is the only part of the brain that continues to function twenty-four hours a day*. All limbic centers participate: the hypothalamic functions ensuring an uninterrupted continuation of the body's vital functions, the septal region and amygdaloid nuclei providing the neuronal energy for the activation of visual engrams via its pathways to the hippocampi (see chap. 10), the various emotional centers that, by way of mnemonic fusions, convey to our dreams an emotional quality.

Moreover, intrinsic pacemakers such as the suprachiasmatic nuclei induce in predictable circadian rhythms the production and secretion of hormones or hormone-releasing or hormone-inhibitory factors such as ACTH, PIF, testosterone, gonadotropic hormones, growth hormone, and thyroid-stimulating hormone in precise circadian rhythms. These hormones affect directly or indirectly drives or emotional states in positive or negative ways. Thyroid-stimulating hormone is known to cause emotional lability or anxiety, while its deficiency may result in depression; ACTH may cause either depression or a euphoric state; testosterone stimulates sexual drives; gonadotropic hormones play a significant psychological role in the premenstrual syndrome (details in chap. 10).

The predictable occurrences of the peaks and valleys of hormonal undulations explain the predictable occurrence of four REM stages of dreaming. Because their fluctuations are not synchronized, as illustrated in figure 8 (p. 117), the four independent REM stages are different in the intensity of dreaming as well as in their distinctive EEG patterns, which range from alpha rhythms in stage 1 to sleep spindles in stage 4, which are correlated with specific hormones.[4]

The limbic system is also connected via a direct pathway with the RAS. This pathway serves the amygdaloid nuclei to alert the RAS in the event of external or imminent threat during the waking states or by means of mnemonic fusions during sleep. This connection may explain the waves of aminergic and cholinergic activities in the RAS observed by Hobson and McCarley, as well as the awakening during nightmarish dreams or the insomnia experienced during manic episodes caused by an overactive limbic system and the "dawning insomnia" experienced in certain types of depression in which the corticosteroid serum levels are elevated.[5] The REM studies of patients suffering from this kind of depression show changes in the REM–non-REM cycle.[6]

Does dreaming serve a particular function? Dreams were to Freud the "royal road to the Unconscious." As mentioned earlier, he conceived of dreams as disguised expressions of "wish-fulfillment" of instinctual (sexual or aggressive) impulses that are repressed during the waking state. He interpreted the usual unintelligibility of dream content as a reflection of an organized process (the "dream work") by which a repressed wish or conflict is condensed, displaced, and/or converted into a symbolic disguise.

Reiser revised these notions with the following three postulates:

1. The mind exploits the unique REM brain state for its own cognitive purposes, including problem solving and related memory functions.
2. The dream process starts with daytime problem-solving concerns. These daytime experiences generate feelings that, in turn, serve to recruit mnemonic images that appear in the dream when the REM states and PGO (pons-geniculate-occipital cortex) waves occur.
3. The unique physiology of the REM brain state provides neural mechanisms for activating the associatively organized mnemonic perceptual image patterns to appear in the dreams and develop into dream events.[7]

Based on the above, Reiser defined dreaming in man as "the subjective experience of vital memory and problem-solving function, made possible by the special psychophysiological condition that obtain mind/brain/body during sleep."[8]

The question remains how the mind noncognitively solves problems during the night that it cannot solve during the day when it is awake. Reiser addressed this issue by means of psychoanalytic principles in his fascinating accounts of patients' revelations during long-term therapy.[9]

A purely biological explanation of dreaming (i.e., without a psychological "purpose") is conceivable in light of the fact that dreaming also appears to occur in animals that are in possession of a brain and thus of a limbic system. Since animals presumably do not suffer from the actions of a superego, their dream states could comfortably be interpreted as a natural consequence of neural impulses ignited by the never-sleeping limbic system and its mnemonic fusions with the visual memory banks.

The notion that the limbic system is the sole source of dreaming in humans as well also allows a neurophysiological explanation of the frequent bizarreness of dream content. During the waking states, we are capable of moving a given transient gestalt from its original global gestalt and implant it into another global gestalt or partially and momentarily "overlap" that gestalt. Our capability of image overlapping has been demonstrated by R. N. Shepard and L. A. Cooper[10] and is illustrated in figure 9. Its frequent occurrence during dreaming reflects the fleeting and random activations of the visual memory banks by different limbic centers, resulting in the confluence of "mismatched" gestalts and the absence of supervision by the sleeping prefrontal cortex. Another contributing factor to kaleidoscopic dream sceneries is the fact that visual engrams are not stored in the memory banks in any categorical system but according to the chronological occurrence of their original visual percepts.

While the above cautions against bold interpretations of dreams as to the "motivations" of the dreamer or dreamster, there is no question about the importance of a scrupulous analysis of the composition of confluent dream gestalts described by patients in psy-

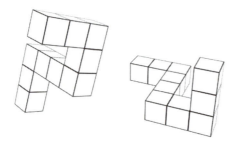

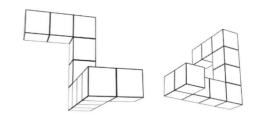

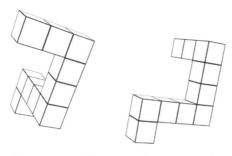

Fig. 9. Establishing which one of the three sets has identical structures demonstrates our capacity to mentally rotate internal images.

chotherapy. As illustrated in Reiser's volume,[11] they may contain glimpses of internal images that remain dormant during the waking states due to the defensive interference of the prefrontal cortex, as discussed in the section of the unconscious.

Whatever benefits future research may uncover with regard to dreaming, in the larger perspective of the central issue of this book, the most important implication of the neurophysiological rationale of dreaming as advanced above is its support for the rationale of the origin and nature of the mind and mental functions, as advanced in previous sections. The fact that dreaming occurs during sleep in the absence of mental functions and the fact that only the functions of the limbic system can explain the irrepressible and precisely timed periodic activation of internal engrams support the notion that the limbic system also serves as the biological generator for the continuous activation of internal images during the waking states, while the simultaneous experiences of visual percepts lend credence to the notion that our experience of the self/nonself/cognition triad is a dialectical product, which explains its absence during sleep.

NOTES

1. E. Aserinsky and N. Kleitman, "Regularly Occurring Periods of Eye Motility and Concurrent Phenomena during Sleep," *Science* 118 (1953): 273–74.

2. R. W. McCarley and J. A. Hobson, "The Neurobiological Origins of Psychoanalytic Dream Theory," *American Journal of Psychiatry* 134 (1977): 1211–21.

3. S. P. Springer and G. Deutsch, *Left Brain, Right Brain*, 2nd ed. (San Francisco: W. H. Freeman, 1985).

4. Moore et al., in *Comprehensive Textbook of Psychiatry*, ed. H. I. Kaplan and B. J. Sadock, 2 vols. (Baltimore: Williams & Wilkins, 1989).

5. E. J. Sacher et al., "Cortisol Production in Depressive Illness," *Archives of General Psychiatry* 23, no. 4 (1970): 289–98.

6. McCarley and Hobson, "Neurobiological Origins," pp. 1211–21.

7. M. F. Reiser, *Memory in Mind and Brain* (New York: Basic Books, 1990).

8. Ibid.

9. M. F. Reiser, *Mind, Brain, Body* (New York: Basic Books, 1984).

10. R. N. Shepard and L. A. Cooper, *Images and Their Transformations* (Cambridge, MA: MIT Press, 1982).

11. Reiser, *Mind, Brain, Body*.

PART 4

BRAIN, MIND, AND BODY

13

THE MIND-BODY PROBLEM

An old rule in medicine has it that there is an inverse correlation between the number of remedies for an ill-defined disease and their therapeutic efficacy. In a somewhat skewed way, this rule comes to mind when one considers the large number and diversity of doctrines that have been advanced through the centuries to remedy the mind-body problem. To illustrate, Mario Bunge begins his volume *The Mind-Body Problem* with a review of forty-nine (!) of the most frequently cited explanatory models.[1] He points out, however, that in spite of the theoretical differences between these models, they all can be categorized as either reflections of the concept of psychophysical monism (mind and body are one) or representations of the Cartesian view of psychophysical dualism (mind and body are independent entities).

Bunge concluded that the core of the mind-body problem is the question: What is the mind? But when we apply the cerebral/empirical concept of the mind, we are confronted with another question. The cerebral/empirical concept suggests that the mind is an empirical epiphenomenon, whereas the body is a material object. This implies that mind and body are distinctively different entities. Yet we do not experience them as independent entities, as René Descartes believed. Without the physical brain, there can be no mind; without the mind, we cannot realize our body as self-object. How, then, do we come to realize our material body as a self-object with our empirical mind?

REALIZING THE BODY AS SELF-OBJECT

We experience our body in two distinctly different ways: as a source of somatoceptive sensations, as discussed in chapter 5, and as a self-object, discussed below.

As the sole determinant of our being, as the exclusive source of our somatoceptive experiences and as the executor or executrix of our contemplated actions to meet our needs, desires, and goals in everyday life, our body is so convincingly our most personal possession that it appears utterly superfluous to raise the question of how we came to realize it as a self-object. However, while the connotation of the widely used term *bodily self* may seem self-evident, the processes by which we develop our notion of the body as self-object have yet to be clarified.

Visually we perceive our body as we perceive all other objects; that is, we form of every visual body percept a visual engram that, when activated, is experienced as a body image. Because of the many different postures we usually assume, and because of the various activities and movements we perform with the different body parts, we form a considerable number of body images. Since our body percepts are inevitable components of our global visual gestalts, their engrams are stored in our primary visual memory bank as part of our global visual percepts. While it is not possible to reproduce all our body images at once, we mentally unify them as components of a separate *conceptual assembly* because they represent the same object, which is (during the wakening states) constantly recognized. This conceptual conglomerate of our body images is synonymous with the term *body concept*.

As discussed in chapter 3, our notions of self and selfness are not based on the observation or experience of tangible qualities but on verbal descriptions of simultaneously experienced dialectical qualities of selfness versus nonself, such as visual mental representations versus actual visual percepts. Similarly, our experiences of our ever-present body and our control of its actions and movements, combined with our continual experiences of proprioceptive and other somatoceptive sensations, are all features that are dialectically opposed to the unpredictable appearances, disappearances, and activities of others. These empirical opposites explain how we experience our body as a self-object.

Our body images not only are the building blocks of our body concept, they contribute to a variety of psychological functions as well. The fact that this role has remained obscure thus far reflects the historical difficulties that have surrounded the definition and use of the term *body image*, as illustrated in the next chapter.

NOTE

1. M. Bunge, *The Mind-Body Problem* (Oxford: Pergamon Press, 1980).

14

BODY IMAGES, DEFINITION, AND STRUCTURES

The term *body image* was introduced in 1935 by P. Schilder in his volume *The Image and Appearance of the Human Body* and has been widely used since then in psychiatry and psychology. It became an integral part of personality theories; it was implicated in the causation of psychiatric conditions and standard procedures for its measurements were developed. However, Schilder's definition of the body image as "the picture of our body which we form in our mind, the way in which the body appears to ourselves, the process by which we experience it as a distinct entity" has continually challenged psychologists, psychiatrists, neurologists, anthropologists, and philosophers.[1] Their definitional efforts resulted in a variety of diverse, often esoteric, formulations, in many of which the term *body image* was interchanged with the terms *body concept, body percept, body schema, body ego,* or *body boundaries.* These unjustifiable interchanges not only reflected what Critchley called "an intolerable chaos" surrounding the term *body image;*[2] they also signified difficulties in the general understanding of how humans perceive and conceive their body.

It was not until 1985 that Christiaan van der Velde questioned the use of "the" body image, as if it were one complete mental representation of our body, and proposed a new interpretation of the term based on four premises, updated as follows.[3]

Premise 1: *Not one but numerous body images.* This premise reflects a departure from the traditional adherence to Schilder's notion of "the" image of the body. Although we *conceptualize* our body as a compact entity, we are not capable of forming one complete image of the body. The limitations of our visual perceptions make it impossible to perceive at one given time all possible phenomenological aspects of our body in their entirety or as a three-dimensional object. Our visual perceptions of our body, direct and indirect (i.e., by way of mirror, photographs, or video recordings) always are restricted to partial views of the body (front, back, side), even when we perceive ourselves in full length.

Furthermore, because of the numerous variations in our movements, postures, and facial expressions, we perceive a given part of our body in different positions, acts, or looks. One's face can show a smile or tears or express anger, bewilderment, or sadness. Consequently, our visual perceptions of our body result in a multitude of independently established body images. (Although vocalizations have never been included in previous definitions of body images, they, too, are somatic activities that produce mental representations, as discussed in chapter 9.)

Not only are we incapable of visually perceiving all our possible bodily features and movements in their entirety; we also are incapable of mentally reproducing all the images we have formed of our body in their entirety. However, thanks to our ability to conceptually realize the relatedness of our body images to the same object, we mentally unify our body images in a conceptual composite that constitutes the foundation of our body concept, which is synonymous with the bodily self.

Premise 2: *Not just bodily reflections.* Body images are not merely mental reflections of our physical self. When their visual engrams are formed, these usually are mnemonically fused with environmental appraisals of and reactions to our appearances and behaviors experienced. These mnemonic fusions thus convey to our body images an environmentally determined psychological meaning. Consequently, our body images are fundamental dynamisms in the development of the qualitative aspects of our self-concept and so contribute to the characteristics of personality.

Premise 3: *We also form body images of others.* The formation of body images is not restricted to the visual perceptions of one's physical self. We also form internal images of our visual perceptions of the appearances and behaviors of others. These body images are designated as extraneous body images. Their perceptual and functional properties are the same as those of our own body images. We perceive others by means of partial and ever-changing appearances, different actions, and changes in physiognomy and thus form of each given individual a multitude of extraneous body images. They cannot be visualized or remembered in their entirety, but we unify them into a conceptual composite representative of each given person. They are also mnemonically fused with our notions of the psychological qualities of others. Therefore, extraneous body images form the foundations of our concepts of the physical and psychological characteristics of others and thus serve as cues for our interpretations of their social behaviors and their nonverbal expression of their physical and emotional feeling states.

Premise 4: *The formation and functions of all body images, of oneself and of others, are the inherent consequences of the following axiomatic roles of the body in human relationships.* (1) Bodily appearances are sine qua non for the occurrence of all human interactions. Be it a simple vocal contact by telephone, the arrival of a newborn, or the repeated contacts during an established relationship, all human encounters begin and end with the appearance and disappearance of the human body. (2) The body is the only medium for all human psychological transactions, verbal or nonverbal.

COMPOSITION OF BODY IMAGES

Body images consist thus of two components:

(1) *a physical component*, which represents the perceived gestalt of a bodily aspect like a face, posture, gesture, or a given motion; and

(2) *a psychological meaning*, which reflects our notion of the feeling, thought, or personal quality associated with each given gestalt, such as someone's kind, stern, warm, and friendly face or someone's angry and threatening fist.

Fig. 10. We can determine someone's mood by a simple change in the mouth.

The physical component of extraneous body images is the basis for our perceptual recognition of others' appearances and actions; their pyschological meaning determines how we interpret their appearances and actions as bodily reflections of their invisible feelings and intentions, as illustrated in these two popular examples from Gestalt psychology (see fig. 10).

The physical component of our own body images is our mental reflections of our bodily characteristics; their psychological meaning reflects our notions of the self-representational effects of our appearances and behaviors upon others. Therefore, our own body images serve as mental blueprints for the designs of our social behaviors: we enthusiastically greet a close friend with wide open arms; we ostentatiously turn our back to someone to display disdain; we produce a friendly smile to express kindness—or to conceal hostile feelings. *Thus, our repertoire of body images, our own and extraneous ones, constitutes our dictionary of nonverbal communication.*

NOTES

1. P. Schilder, *The Image and Appearance of the Human Body* (New York: International Universities Press, 1950).

2. M. Critchley, *The Divine Banquet of the Brain* (New York: Raven Press, 1980).

3. C. van der Velde, "Body Images of One's Self and of Others: Developmental and Clinical Significance," *American Journal of Psychiatry* 142, no. 5 (1985): 527–37.

15

PSYCHOLOGICAL FUNCTIONS OF EXTRANEOUS BODY IMAGES

There are several reasons for elaborating on extraneous body images before discussing the psychological functions of our own body images. Extraneous body images are the first functional body images formed in life; they are the first psychological instruments that enable the infant and young child to "read" the appearances and intentions of human objects and thus mediate the development of the most crucial foundation of all future interpersonal interactions and relationships: basic trust and attachment (see chap. 6). Furthermore, extraneous body images are the first mental representations of external transient objects necessary for the development of the self/nonself/cognition triad and simultaneously form the mental "building blocks" of his or her concept of others. Finally, a review of their psychological functions will facilitate the discussion of the psychological functions of our own body images.

There is no era in human life that so clearly radiates the psychological importance of extraneous body images than the first few years, when verbal communication has yet to develop and the infant's capacity to "read" environmental intentions is dependent solely on his or her extraneous body images. Their interpretative potentials are determined by the mnemonic fusions formed between extraneous body images and the various pleasurable somatoceptive and emotional sensations caused by the mother's ministrations and repertoire of touching, stroking, rocking, cuddling, bathing, and minimassages. Because of these neurophysiological connections, extraneous body images are permanent mnemonic units that exert their psychological functions not only during the nonverbal and noncognitive stages of development but throughout life. They are the lasting instruments that tell the infant, the growing child, and adolescent that he or she is worth the environment's attention and care and love, and assist the eventual adult to correctly interpret others in their interactions.

Furthermore, continual and consistent exteroceptive stimulation and the consequent development of extraneous body images during the first year of life are prerequisites for the unfolding of the brain's potential for development, even in infrahuman species. V. H. Denenberg et al. demonstrated that reduced stimulation of young rats impedes their learning capacity, as is evident from the loss of dendrites and morphological abnormalities in the brain.[1] In contrast, the administration of certain agents such as thyroid hormone proved to increase the capacity for learning and to cause an increase in brain size. When kittens (which are naturally blind for the first nine postnatal days) are deprived of light stimuli for more than three months following birth, they will have permanently lost their potential to see.[2] Many other studies have confirmed that the capacity of the brain to multiply neurons and dendrites and to form new synapses, that is, mnemonic fusions, is contingent upon exteroceptive stimulation and that this stimulation must occur within a given period of time (one year for the human infant, shorter for other species).[3] If exteroceptive stimulation is withheld or reduced during this "critical" period of development, the brain will lose its innate but time-bound potential to grow in size and function.

The above explains the deleterious effects of maternal deprivation or neglect during infancy. When a caregiver's interactions with an infant are insufficient, inadequate, or emotionally uninvolved, bonding and attachment will not take place. Such infants show an irreversible lack of intellectual functions, social responsiveness, and social skills.[4]

The importance of the formation and continued experience of extraneous body images during early infancy becomes apparent later in infancy and childhood when the infant is deprived of earlier meaningful interactions with the mother. R. Spitz reported in 1965 the results of his observations of 170 "well-cared-for" infants who had been placed in an orphanage between the ages of six to twelve months.[5] Even though all infants were timely fed and diapered by competent nursing staff, they all developed manifestations of a depressed state (incessant crying, clinging, weight loss), which Spitz called "anaclitic" (i.e., psychologically dependent) depression.

THE FORMATION OF OUR CONCEPT OF OTHERS

It is puzzling why none of the many theories of personality development (including object relations theories) has addressed the question of how children or adults form their concept of the personality of others. All theories on child development portray parental figures as givens whose personal qualities are somehow available for the infant's or child's "identification" to serve him or her as molds for the formation of his or her own personality. However, these theories do not explain how the rudimentary perceptual and cognitive capacities during infancy and childhood enable the infant or child to recognize human objects as objects or how they identify with these objects and internalize their good and bad qualities. For example, a still frequently cited theory is the individuation-separation concept, which M. S. Mahler presumed to take place some time during the middle of the first year: "in the beginning the infant views the mother as part of himself. But, little by little, experience by experience, the infant realizes that the mother is not part of him nor is he the part of the mother. This realization is the beginning of the infant's development of individuality."[6]

Contrary to these assumptions, it appears that, as an inherent consequence of the child's own progressive stages of perceptual and cognitive maturation and the dialectical differentiation between self and nonself, human objects from the child's "view" become persons, physically and psychologically. This involves a gradually unfolding process of (1) forming internal object representations (by means of extraneous body images) and (2) the personification of these objects, which results from the simultaneously experienced somatoceptive and emotional sensations evoked by the external objects' appearances and actions. To illustrate the progression of the infant's and child's perceptual and cognitive skills, I follow the developmental cognitive outline of Piaget.[7]

SENSORIMOTOR PERIOD (BIRTH TO EIGHTEEN MONTHS)

As described earlier, Piaget demonstrated that the dawning of human operational intelligence becomes apparent by the end of the sensori-motor period in the form of the first basic invariant of all human knowledge: the awareness of object permanence. The infant's begin-ning awareness of the existence of objects "out there" indicates that he or she has developed the capacity to activate internal visual images and thus experiences extraneous body images. This awareness should not suggest that the infant has internally formed complete object rep-resentations. R. Spitz, D. N. Stern, and others have shown that the infant's internal representations of the mother during the first year of the sensorimotor period are partial and independent representations of her physical features and actions.[8] Furthermore, in contrast with the presentational constancy of inanimate objects (on which Piaget's conclusions were based), human object presentations are character-ized by continual changes in appearance, actions, facial expressions, and vocalizations that the child mnemonically stores in a growing number and variety as his perceptual development progresses. Con-sequently, the child's eventual mental construct of each human object consists of a continually expanding assembly of related extra-neous body images representing a given human object.

PREOPERATIONAL STAGE (TWO TO SEVEN YEARS)

The preoperational child begins to show an intuitive notion of unity of the various presentations of each human object. Yet the imme-diacy and specificity of his thinking and the still-limited file of visual engrams confine his perceptions of a human object to each of its momentary appearances.

CONCRETE OPERATIONS (SEVEN TO ELEVEN YEARS)

It requires the unfolding of the child's ability of reflective abstraction (scanning his expanding files of visual engrams) and conversation during this stage of development to lend to his thinking the necessary mobility and reversibility to realize that the appearances of others are only partial and transient manifestations.

FORMAL OPERATIONS (ELEVEN TO FIFTEEN YEARS)

The unfolding of formal thinking reflects the adolescent's ability to conceptually unify the numerous extraneous body images he has accumulated of each human object, which are mnemonically fused with the representative linguistic engrams. The resulting conceptual composites of extraneous body images belonging to a given human objects enable the adolescent to experience others as "whole" persons in spite of their partial and perpetually changing appearances and also explain the awareness during each encounter that there is always more than meets the eye.

PERSONIFICATION OF HUMAN OBJECTS

While the attribution of personal qualities to each human object begins with the earliest human interactions by means of mnemonic attachments of somatoceptive and emotional sensations to extraneous body images, personification of a human object per se begins following the child's development of linguistic understanding and related abstractive abilities. The appearances of others are now perceived in combination with their verbalizations of their feelings and intentions. These verbal communications have two effects. First, they make the child aware of inner states of others, which initiates the process of personification. Second, these verbal communications are internalized as auditory engrams, which are mnemonically fused with the visual engrams of the simultaneously perceived physical presentations and thus confer on the resulting extraneous body images an interpretative meaning. Consequently, the smiles of others, their frowns, tears, laughter, shouting, and all other physiognomic appearances become for the child symbols of the invisible physical and emotional feelings of others whose expressions he thus learns to "read" by means of his extraneous body images. (This capacity is known as *prosody*.)

Even though language is indispensable for the initiation of the personification process and becomes increasingly important as a means of communication, it is the combination of verbal and non-verbal communications that determine the child's eventual notions of the personal characteristics of each human object. For example, while most parents verbally express their love for their child in various terms, children often observe that parents' attitudes and actions reflect more concern for the feelings and opinions of others. Or a child is invited to climb on mother's lap for a cozy cuddling yet is pushed away for wrinkling mother's dress. Even if the child is spared these "double-bind" experiences in earlier life,[9] sooner or later he or she will discover during the interactions with peers at school or socially that actions speak louder than words and are the most reliable indicators of others' feelings, intentions, and personal qualities.

Finally, certain individual qualities such as kindness, patience, tolerance, cruelty, and aggressiveness are apparent only from physical presentations and actions, while nonverbal behaviors can relate feelings and intentions where words fail: a gentle touch; a reproachful glance; a cold, punitive voice; a prolonged intimate embrace; or the tenderness in a voice, all containing messages that are beyond description, to be understood only by means of the experientially established meaning of corresponding extraneous body images.

ADULT INTERACTIONS

Because extraneous body images are the sole carriers of the memories of all past interpersonal experiences, they mediate the influence of past interactions on all future relationships and interactions, new or old. An unknown individual can turn us on or off during the first encounter by his or her mere physical appearance. Someone's habitus; ways of moving, looking, or smiling; mustache; beard; eye color; hairstyle; or tone of voice or any other bodily feature that resembles characteristics of parents or other significant persons inevitably activate corresponding extraneous body images and thus arouse, consciously or unconsciously, pleasurable or displeasurable memories, which then may influence our reactions and attitude toward the newly met individual. So do our extraneous body images affect our choice of friends or marital partner; they are the basis for the occurrence of transference and countertransference in the psychotherapeutic process; they create the longing for the return of a love object so as to reactivate previous experiences; they preoccupy our thinking during our grief following the loss of a love object and may, as the object's lasting memories, permanently influence future behavior, as illustrated by Nemiah:

> [A] 74-year-old remarkably preserved woman was hospitalized for a depression following the death of her second husband. She had a similar depression after the divorce from her first husband 21 years earlier. Both husbands had been extremely cruel and abusive and were alcoholics. When asked how she could have lived with these men for so long she replied: "But they had such cute black eyes and wavy hair, just like my father." The patient had been deeply attached to her father who passed away when she was 15 years old.[10]

EFFECTS ON INDIVIDUAL BEHAVIOR

Extraneous body images also play a significant role in the shaping of an individual's own personality. To the growing child, extraneous body images are his most utilized "toys." As the mnemonic residues of his perceptions of others, they serve as mental models that enable the child to play his daily games of imitation and role playing. The physical components (i.e., their gestalts) enable him or her to imitate behaviors of father or mother; their psychological meanings enable him or her to mentally act out their "good" or "bad" personal qualities and social roles as he perceived them. Whichever component is acted out, each is because of the reciprocity of their mnemonic fusions inextricably experienced with the other component.

The child's mental and physical imitations of his or her extraneous body images facilitate several processes which are in all theories of personality development considered crucial for the child's psychological and behavioral growth. They enable the child to reenact past interactions with an imitated object and thus to mentally reexperience pleasurable or displeasurable events and so modify the latter in a coping way. They facilitate the child's distinctions between the characteristic bodily and psychological aspects of the different members in the family setting and thus furnish the foundation of the child's first notions of social roles and gender identities. They promote the child's adoption of the behavioral characteristics of parents and other significant individuals (such as teachers and national heroes) by incorporating the extraneous body images formed of them into his or her own repertory of behaviors. Extraneous body images are, thus, the transmitters of the environmental familial, social, and cultural idiosyncrasies onto the child's own mental attitudes and behaviors.

While the child's incorporation of environmental behaviors usually is the consequence of the child's pleasurable memories associated with these behaviors, there are situations in which behaviors are imitated and incorporated even though they are mnemonically fused with negative associations. For example, psychiatric studies have shown that the abusive behavior of a parent may be imitated and eventually incorporated so as to "please" the parent and hopefully avoid further abuse. Such behavioral incorporation is known as *identification with the aggressor* and considered to be a psychological defense mechanism. However, R. Blanck and G. Blanck emphasized the confusion about the distinction between identification, incorporation, introjection, and internalization.[11]

The term *incorporation* is used here as the permanent inclusion of certain behaviors of others into one's own repertoire of behaviors (i.e., becoming a component of one's own body images). *Internalization* is used in this volume as the inclusion of the ideas, beliefs, and values of others into one's linguistic memory banks. Freud considered identification synonymous with "becoming like some one else." Not only has such transformation never been explained, it is an impossible psychological maneuver in a normally functioning mind in view of the indispensable self-nonself differentiation for normal cognitive functions. It can occur only in delusional conditions.

Yet object relations theories consider identification with parental figures a fundamental process through which the development of self and personality evolves in children and even in infants. Blanck and Blanck proposed that identification is more adequately described as the process by which object representations are transferred to self-representations (which is in actuality incorporating extraneous body images into the repertoire of one's own body images). They further emphasize that the dual usage of identification as a defense mechanism and as a normal developmental process is unacceptable. The following anecdote also illustrates the need for clarification of the term.

Freud was consulted for an epidemic of fainting spells in a young women's boarding school in Freiburg, Switzerland. A student had received a love letter and reacted with a fainting spell. Soon a series of fainting spells spread among other students. Freud interpreted this epidemic as an example of "histrionic identification" with the unconscious meaning "we would like to get love letters, too."

With whom or what did identification take place? For what defensive reason? Considering the proclivity of female adolescents for romance and drama combined with a strong desire for social recognition, it is hard to dismiss the possibility that these fainting spells simply reflected how useful extraneous body images are for making a social statement where words would not do: "I, too, received a love letter."

The notion of identification as "becoming someone else" is in conflict with the dialectical sense of self versus nonself. It can be observed in psychotic (delusional) conditions. Using the self/nonself/cognition triad, identification is an intellectual process of realizing someone else's physical or emotional pain by means of extraneous body images without actually experiencing the other's feelings. This realization requires the possession of related extraneous body images that are associated with one's experience of pain either by personal experience or intellectual projections. Even when actual feelings are experienced, as in empathy and sympathy, one does not lose one's identity.

—•—

What are the extraneous body images others form of us? This question leads us to the psychological functions of our own body images.

NOTES

1. V. H. Denenberg et al., "Infantile Stimulation Induced Brain Lateralization in Rats," *Science* 201 (1978): 1150–51.

2. D. H. Hubel, *Eye, Brain, and Vision* (New York: Scientific American Library/Freeman, 1988).

3. G. Lynch, *Synapses, Circuits, and the Beginning of Memory* (Cambridge, MA: MIT Press, 1986).

4. L. J. Stone, H. T. Smith, and L. B. Murphy, *The Competent Infant* (New York: Basic Books, 1973).

5. R. Spitz, *First Year of Life* (New York: International Universities Press, 1965).

6. M. S. Mahler, F. Pine, A. Bergman, *The Psychological Birth of the Human Infant* (New York: Basic Books, 1975).

7. J. L. Philips, *The Origin of Intellect* (San Francisco: Freeman, 1969).

8. Spitz, *The First Year of Life*; D. N. Stern, *The Interpersonal World of the Infant* (New York: Basic Books, 1985).

9. M. M. Berger, *Beyond the Double Bind* (New York: Brunner/Mazel, 1978).

10. J. C. Nemiah, *Foundations of Psychopathology* (New York: J. Aronson, 1973).

11. R. Blanck and G. Blanck, *Beyond Ego Psychology* (New York: Columbia University Press, 1986).

16

PSYCHOLOGICAL FUNCTIONS OF IMAGES OF THE BODILY SELF

One of the intriguing phenomena in human psychological development is the sequence of the formation and utilization of one's own body images: their psychological meaning is internalized and utilized before the actual corresponding physical appearances have been perceived.

In the normally developing child, visual perceptions of the body generally are incidental and fleeting operations until mid-latency or adolescence, when physical appearances become the subject of intense study.* Yet from the very beginning of the child's linguistic understanding, he is continuously made aware of environmental opinions of his physical characteristics and actions. He is told by parents, their friends, neighbors, and relatives about his looks; he is commended for his helpful, considerate, polite, cute behavior or reprimanded for his laziness or mischievous and selfish acts. These appraisals have two fundamental impacts on the child's psychological and social development.

First, they provide the child with an empirical framework of behaviors and postures that enable him to please (or provoke) others, avoid punishment, or attract attention or reward. Second,

---

*Dream studies have established that children do not begin to "see" themselves bodily in dreams before the age of eight.

they make him aware of whether and why he is loved, liked, or disliked and what he means to others and thus provide the child with a beginning sense of personal identity. Because these earliest appraisals are prompted exclusively by the child's physical appearances and activities, the child's beginning sense of self-identity is inseparably associated with his empirical framework of demeanor.

During the elementary school years, every child learns that such bodily features as height, obesity, strength, coordination, complexion, and looks are used with often painful accuracy by peers, classmates, teachers, and coaches in the determination of the pecking order in social and athletic activities. Bodily "flaws" become social liabilities and ever-present potential for rejection and humiliation; outstanding physical features and abilities become assets that provide gateways to friendships, admiration, and peer-group acceptance. Thus, when the child approaches the end of latency and is about to embark on the actual study of bodily aspects and capabilities, the child is inevitably aware of the fact that physical characteristics are "social markers" of his or her personality.

The perceptual completion of the formation of his own body images begins full scale following the child's entry into the brave new world of adolescence. The pubertal changes in his physique, his unfolding ability of formal abstract thinking and subsequent capacity for self-reflection mark the beginning of an extreme self-consciousness, psychologically and physically. Much time is spent before the mirror to analyze the shape and features of the body: form of nose, ears, chin, and teeth and the proportions of arms, legs, muscles, chest, and buttock. He repeatedly checks what is "right" or what looks odd, what he likes and what he would like to change or to get rid of. He tries out various postures, movements, different hairstyles, and imitations of others, using his extraneous body images of his favorite heroes to explore what self-representational success they may have for him.

The adolescent's visual self-studies result in an ever-growing accumulation of body images, each presenting a different perception of a given part of the bodily self. Although he is incapable of visualizing all mental representations of his physical self in their entirety, his developing abilities of conceptualization enable him to conceptually unify them into a composite of body images.

In summary, humans' formation of body images has two psychological consequences. First, because one's own body images are not only the mental representations of the physical self but also inextricably associated with one's pychological qualities, they are in the most comprehensive sense of the term *self-images*, as detailed in chapter 11. Second, because body images are the mental mirrors of one's physical self-presentations and the personal self-representational effects upon others, they serve as mental blueprints for the designs of social behaviors and interactions, as illustrated in the next chapter.

17

THE HUMAN ENCOUNTER
Another Dialectical Event

Human encounters represent another set of dialectical events: one's encounters with others are only possible because of others' encounters with him. As a consequence of the inherent mutuality of bodily appearances during each human interaction, and the inevitable awareness of each participant of being appraised as he appraises the other, no individual can dissociate his projections of the effects of his appearances on others from his notions that others are engaged in interpreting him.

Few events can better illustrate one's dialectical use of body images than the interactions between an actor and his audience during a stage performance. The actor's task is to make his audience believe that he feels and thinks as his role demands. Obviously, this cannot be accomplished by an announcement to the audience that the actor is supposed to be, for example, in a state of sadness. The very art of acting is the portrayal of human psychological states by means of bodily appearances and actions and intonations of speech. Accordingly, the actor lags onto the stage, head and shoulders stooped, facial expression desolate, voice tired and indifferent. He anticipates that these physical presentations will be perceived by the audience as reflections of inner sadness because he would make such interpretation if he were among the audience. At the conclusion of his performance, the audience responds with carefully measured lukewarm or thunderous applause, confident that the intensity of the applause will convey to the actor its opinion of the excellence or mediocrity of his performance.

In the everyday theater of human life, all people use their body images as actors do. We exchange formalities or genuine feelings, disguise motives, or pretend concern by converting our own body images into perceivable physical presentations to be interpreted by others according to the appearance and actions selected: an approving nod, a questioning frown, an emphatic look. We smile away a feeling of embarrassment, we camouflage feelings of hostility with an appearance of kindness or courtesy lest we jeopardize a personal or professional relationship. Men rise to their feet upon a woman's entrée to show their respect and good manners or just to show that they know what politeness is. The engaging smiles of campaigning politicians; their cordial, generous handshakes and emphatic pats on shoulders; their hugging and kissing children and babies to present to voters the picture of a philanthropist are classical examples of the dialectical use of body images.

SOCIAL MANAGEMENT

Body images are thus indispensable devices for the management of social behavior. They enable a person to project how others see him by means of his appearances and actions; they serve him to selectively control the establishment and preservation of a desirable view of them selves; and they enable them to create within others impressions that do not precisely reflect his actual self. Examples of the voluminous literature on the intriguing ways humans manage their unavoidably perceptible bodily self-presentations are listed in the footnote below.

Ideally, one's appearances and behaviors should be true reflections of one's psychological states. Freud suggested: "to be completely honest with oneself (and with others, I may add) is the best effort a human being can make."

However, most people do not wish to disclose every aspect of their actual inner self. Many people often disguise certain feelings or intentions by feigning different ones. While the invisibility of the psychological self affords one virtually unlimited verbal claims regarding his inner states, his bodily appearances and actions are unconcealable self-reflections that are continuously subject to the scrutiny of others during every encounter. Therefore, it is imperative that one's physical presentations and behaviors corroborate one's verbal communications, or, when social interactions are strictly nonverbal, clearly portray the selected inner state.

Thus, one's ability to effectively utilize his repertoire of body images is an absolute necessity for the successful management of his social interactions. Without proper facial expressions, movements, gestures, postures, and vocal inflections, one cannot convince others of his feelings of friendliness, respect, admiration, or love. The malingerer cannot solicit empathy without showing "obvious" bodily signs of physical or emotional distress. Even a well-integrated individual who has come to terms with himself and others occasionally must employ his body images to pretend, for example, considerateness or to substantiate the genuineness of his verbally expressed empathy.

DIALECTICAL UNCERTAINTIES

A most remarkable aspect of human encounters is the fact that even though an individual's body is his or her most personally owned property, its self-representational characteristics are better known to others than to himself or herself. While a person has a clear perception of others and others of him, he cannot perceive himself as others do. Owing to his body images he is capable of projecting how his presentations may be perceived by others; he has no certainty, however, that his appearances are interpreted according to his projections. Although the verbal and nonverbal responses of others provide him with clues to assess the possible effects of his presentations, others' opinions differ from person to person (because of the strictly personal meanings of their extraneous body images), and he cannot always be sure whether their responses reflect their actual opinions.

There is no reconciliation for these dialectical uncertainties. Every individual must rely upon his or her own judgment and intuitions in determining whether his or her appearances and behaviors are interpreted according to his or her projections.

While these uncertainties are a potential source of discomfort to many individuals, they also have two positive aspects. First, the uncertain receptions of one's presentations create an element of challenge and excitement to one's social interactions, particularly new encounters. Second, they accentuate the joy of such special relationships as an intimate friendship, marriage, or an unfolding love relationship, when dialectical concerns dissipate in a mutual, unconditional acceptance of one's verbal and nonverbal self-expressions.

A good number of individuals are dissatisfied with some of their physical characteristics and employ various means to improve their appearances and spend fortunes on hairdressers, cosmetics, and attire, expertly guided by the crafty creators of advertisements and commercials, who might not be in business if it were not for people's body images.

Humans' concerns with physical appearances do not diminish with age, for the formation of body images is a ceaseless process throughout life. The perception of the physical changes brought about by the inevitable process of involution result in new body images that render old familiar body images as pleasant but unusable memories, which lead to rearrangements of one's bodily appearances. The integration of graying hair, balding, wrinkling skin, or faltering bodily functions is an unpleasant task and in many cases calls for toupees, rejuvenating exercises, plastic surgery, and an abundance of makeup.[1]

— • —

How do we effectively convert our mental body images into physical behaviors? How do we control our physical self-representations during our interactions when we are unable to observe ourselves while other have a front-row look at us? How do we accomplish such perfect synchronizations between our self-invisible facial expressions, our gestures, vocal inflections, and our feelings and thoughts?

NOTE

1. J. Benthall and T. Polhemus, *The Body as a Medium of Expression* (New York: E. P. Dutton, 1975); P. Bull, *Body Movement and Interpersonal Communication* (New York: John Wiley & Sons, 1983); P. Ekman and W. V. Friesen, *Unmasking the Face* (Englewood Cliffs, NJ: Prentice-Hall, 1975); R. G. Harper, A. N. Wiends, and J. D. Matarazzo, eds., *Nonverbal Communication: The State of the Art* (New York: Wiley, 1978); R. P. Harrison, *Beyond Words* (Englewood Cliffs, NJ: Prentice-Hall, 1974); S. Jourard, *Self-Disclosure: An Experimental Analysis of the Transparent Self* (New York: Wiley Interscience, 1971); D. A. Karp and W. C. Yoels, *Symbols, Selves and Society* (New York: J. B. Lippincott, 1979); J. P. Spiegel and P. Machotka, *Messages of the Body* (New York: Free Press, 1974).

18

MIND-BODY INTERACTIONS

In the *Fundamentals of Neurophysiology*, Robert F. Schmidt wrote: "Practically nothing is known of how our mental decisions on posture and movements are converted into bodily actions. Such conversion of thinking and intent into cortical impulses remains, for the time being, far beyond the limits of our understanding."[1]

Gloomy as Schmidt's view may appear, he does accentuate the very problem of mind-body interactions: How do we transform our non-material ideas, wishes, and plans into physical motor actions by means of cortical impulses? The combination of the cerebral/empirical model of mental experiences and the now well-established anatomy and neurophysiology of the motor cortex make it possible to address this question, including other issues raised by O. G. Meyer and K. Roth.[2]

In all vertebrates, motor actions originate in the cortical motor area, which is situated in the frontal lobe immediately anterior of the central sulcus (see fig. 11). It consists in humans of three main regions: the *primary* motor cortex (Brodmann's area four), the *premotor* cortex divided in areas six and eight, and the *secondary* motor area (forty-four), which lies below areas four, six, and eight at the base of the precentral gyrus adjacent to the secondary somatic sensory area (forty-three), which lies at the base of the postcentral gyrus. The primary and premotor cortices are, like the primary and secondary somatic sensory areas, somatotopically arranged.

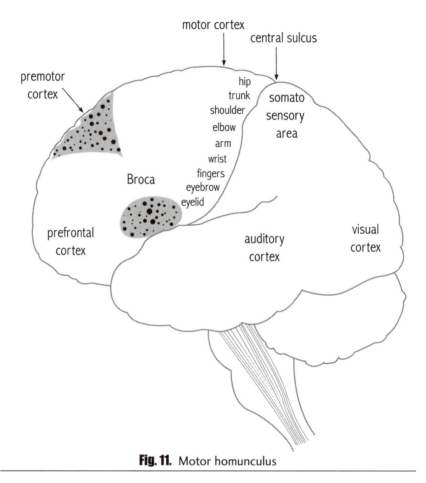

Fig. 11. Motor homunculus

Electrical stimulation (applied in vivo with humans by Penfield and in infrahuman species by Mishkin and Appenzeller) and numerous laboratory studies by Mountcastle, G. Lynch, and others have established the following distribution in functions:

- *Area four* activates distal limb musculature for skilled and delicate movements.
- *The lateral part of area six* controls the activities of the proximal and axial musculature and the orientation of movements toward targets.

- *The medial portion of area six* is usually referred to as the supplementary area and is involved in the programming and storage of complex motor patterns and the sequence of movements.
- *Area eight* is primarily involved in conjugate eye movements.[2]

The function of the secondary motor area (forty-four) is unknown. A possible function is suggested in the section in psychosomatics in chapter 20.

To employ this anatomical knowledge in our effort to understand the dynamics of mind-brain interactions, we first need to address the question: Which source or process induces our motor areas to activate muscle contraction?

GENERATING MOTOR ACTIONS

The answer proposed below was conceived by exploring the fact that the capacity of producing self-invisible motor activities by humans cited at the end of the last chapter is also exercised by infrahuman species. Seagulls take off and land with flawless precision; horses orchestrate four independently moving legs into a perfectly coordinated gallop; dolphins carry out precisely measured somersaults—yet none of these animals visually perceives its own actions and none is known to develop the capacity of epistemological cognition.

All species employ characteristic moving patterns (birds fly, reptiles crawl, fish swim, kangaroos leap, and humans are destined to walk) that reflect anatomical and morphological differences. But in all species, the execution of motor actions involves the same principle, namely, the contraction of musculature, which is in all vertebrates the function of the motor cortex. And so does the human infant, years before the emergence of the dialectical cognition/selfness/consciousness triad, unfold in predictable sequence a specific repertoire of motor actions: smiling, sitting up, crawling, standing, then walking, all without mental preparation for any of these bodily activities. These predictable developments and utilization of motor activities under mindless conditions in all species afford the following conclusions:

(1) All species are born with infrastructured motor areas, which are connected with specific muscular structures.

(2) The mind is not essential to the origination of our motor activities.

(3) Because all animal activities are reflections of the self-pre-serving and species-procreating functions of the limbic system, the only conceivable source of motor activation is the limbic system.

These conclusions are consistent with the occurrence of motor activities evoked by Penfield's electrical stimulation of the motor cortex of patients during brain surgery, following the electrical stimulation of various centers or nuclei in the limbic system of animals, and with the naturally occurring activities by animals. For example, when an animal experiences hunger, the animal, "driven" by neuronal discharges in the feeding center (the perifornical region of the lateral hypothalamus), gets up and searches for food or prey. This search continues until satiation, whereupon the paraventricular nucleus in the medial hypothalamus inhibits the feeding center from firing.[4]

The motor activities in animals are not restricted to their innate setup. During developmental maturation, the originally innate one-to-one connections between the limbic system and primary motor cortex are gradually employed in more complicated actions that are programmed and stored in the premotor areas six and eight (the supplementary motor cortex) by forming specific neuronal constructs that are conveniently labeled as "behavioral templates." For instance, a grizzly bear cub does not instinctively know how to catch a salmon. It starts out slapping and slowly "learns" to pin down or scoop.

The neuronal consolidation into permanent behavioral templates can be explained as the result of N-CAMs, as described in chapter 7. This consolidation also includes the mnemonic fusions formed by means of an extensive network of reciprocal association pathways with visual engrams stored in the occipital association cortex and with somatoceptive memories stored in the parietal cortex. The primary motor cortex also is connected via a direct neural pathway with the limbic system, where it derives the impulses to activate muscular contraction.

The above neurophysiological scenario also applies to the human infant. When the infant experiences hunger pangs, the innate defensive limbic system initiates the infant's crying until the mother appears to ministrate her comforting actions to the infant, who often stops crying by just the sight of the mother.

The *anticipation* of pleasurable sensations also generates motor activities on a sheer neurophysiological basis. A twelve-month-old infant is placed on the floor in the playroom and after a few moments spots the toy box. The infant then crawls to the box, looks inside, and retrieves his or her favorite toy. Piaget conceived this display of the infant's "awareness of object permanence" as the first manifestation of cognition that enables this apparently well-planned undertaking. However, the capacity of cognition does not yet exist at that stage of development and thus calls for a different explanation. When the infant experiences the visual percept of the toy box, this percept activates its corresponding internal image whose global gestalt also contains the transient gestalt of his or her favorite toy. The internal sight of the favorite toy activates the mnemonically fused sense of pleasure. The activation of the associated limbic center transmits its neural discharge to area four (the primary motor cortex), which then "moves" the infant, guided by the global gestalt of the internal image, to the toy box.

This illustration exemplifies the limbic origin of "motivation" and reveals the source of energy that induces by means of electrical discharge the primary motor cortex to activate muscle contractions. It also implicates a role of mental images in the organization of motor activities. This role is not restricted to the naive stages of infancy but applies to the adult mind-brain interactions as well.

THE ROLE OF MENTAL IMAGES

M. Jeannerod concluded his *Cognitive Neuroscience of Action*[5] (which contains a wealth of information for researchers and theoreticians on behavioral control) with a detailed exposition of the problems and theories regarding the formation of cerebral representations of motor actions, the mental preparation and executions of movements, and whether their initiation requires conscious intent. The concepts advanced below may clarify some of these problems.

The contents of mental representations of our physical activities (i.e., body images) are mnemonically fused with emotional memories by means of the hippocampi (see chap. 10) and with a corresponding behavior template in the supplementary motor cortex. The thought of a given activity activates the corresponding template in the supplementary premotor cortex (as demonstrated by way of brain-imaging technology) upon which the supplementary cortex activates the corresponding neuronal module in the somatotopically organized primary cortex. If the aroused area in the limbic system is positive and acceptable, the limbic system summons the primary motor cortex, which then activates the appropriate musculature. If the original thought of action is associated with questionable consequences, the resulting concern or anxiety induces the amygdaloid nuclei to inhibit the execution of the intended action by means of its neural connection with the prefrontal cortex, which, in turn, is neurally connected with the primary cortex, as detailed in chapter 10.

We may, then, distinguish two categories of motor activities: (1) autonomously occurring actions serving survival needs (food, defense, shelter), which are directly induced by activities in the hypothalamus, amygdaloids, and septal region; it is conceivable that these three areas employ area forty-four to reach the primary motor cortex, and (2) mentally induced actions that are subject to our internal (image) inspection of their consequences and controlled by the prefrontal cortex.

While we cannot mentally retrieve our behavioral templates, our body images are mentally reproducible. This reproducibility not only enables us to selectively produce self-invisible motor actions, they contribute to the formation of new complex behavioral templates as well: for example, the executions of the gold medal–winning triple somersault from the ten-meter diving board during the

2000 Olympic Games. Such dives are learned in sequence, induced by mentally projecting the body tumbling between the springboard and the water. Once he has jumped off the springboard and is airborne, the diver then "folds" his body forward to unfold after one rotation to safely land in the water. Repetitions of this single somersault results in the diver's "feel" for the right jumping height, the velocity of folding, and the timing for the unfolding. The memories of all these sensations are synaptically fused and stored in the supplemental premotor cortex, basal ganglia, and the proprioceptive regions in the secondary somatoceptive cortex.

To learn the technique of the double somersault, the diver prepares himself by internally activating the image of his diving body, then he jumps with increased energy for a higher jump and faster rotation. With continued practice, he eventually masters the double, followed by the same preparations for the triple. The required stimulation for the actual contraction originates in the limbic system, which is incited by the "thrill" of diving or by the anticipated joy of winning a gold medal. The same applies to the competitive gymnast's or ballerina's execution of complex combinations of movements by internal commands and internal vision.

Even when the capacity for cognition has been fully established, adults are continuously engaged in numerous activities without having to issue specific mental instructions. Every morning upon awakening, we arise, begin our routine of showering and getting dressed, then move to the kitchen for breakfast, using motor activities without actually thinking about them yet performing them in perfect sequence, reflecting the existence of programmed behavior patterns and the autonomous activations by the limbic system.

The precise and goal-directed execution of such learned motor actions as catching a salmon by infrahuman species can be explained only by the existence of permanently formed behavioral templates, the visual perception of a salmon, the mnemonic fusion between the visual memory (engram) and its behavioral template, and the driving force of the aroused limbic system. Thus, motor actions do not require conscious intentions but do require the existence of a cerebral representation (i.e., engram) of previously perceived external objects whose recurring perception leads to the activation of mnemonically fused behavioral template.

In addition to unconscious (automated) activities such as consuming a meal, humans also are capable of mentally reproducing previous movements by means of body images. The existence of mnemonic fusions with corresponding behavioral templates is apparent during brain imaging from the metabolic activity in the motor cortex when subjects "think" of given actions. While the various centers in the limbic system generate the (electrical) energy for all activities, the multiple connections of each center with multiple body images and as many behavioral templates, a regulatory agent is required to suppress unrelated templates. This regulatory task is the function of the prefrontal cortex, which in humans also inhibits activities that are associated with undesirable consequences. This control involves the neural connections between the amygdaloid nuclei and the prefrontal cortex and neural pathways between the latter and premotor as detailed in chapter 10. As a final corroboration of the role of internal images in the preparation and execution of motor actions, I briefly describe two special categories of motor actions: speech and writing.

SPEECH AND WRITING

As detailed in chapter 9, we store auditory engrams in Wernicke's area, where neural fibers of the arcuate fasciculus connect with Broca's speech center (areas forty-four and forty-five), situated in 95 percent of all humans in the infrafrontal gyrus of the left hemisphere (see fig. 11). Broca's speech area is an association area where coordinated neuronal programs are formed, which I named *verbal templates*. These programs control articulation through the sequencing of the musculature, which employ vocal cords, tongue, lips, and larynx. They are then transmitted to the motor areas four and six to result in spoken language.

Speaking words is a combination of hearing and internal seeing. While talking we internally hear ourselves talk and so check the correct choice of words. The choice of words begins with a "search" of our linguistic visual memory bank. Linguistic engrams are, via connecting pathways, mnemonically fused with auditory engrams. When activated, these auditory engrams activate via the arcuate fasciculus to Broca's center, usually in the left premotor cortex, to actualize corresponding verbal templates as conceived for our motor actions (see fig. 8, p. 117). The formation of verbal templates follows the same scenario described for behavioral templates. During the very early stages after birth, the infant's cries for food when hungry or for other comfort involves innate pathways connecting the limbic system with the lateral area six then gradually an ever-extending number of sounds. During the early schooling of writing (at six and seven years), linguistic engrams (Dick, Jane, and Spot) are, during their formation, mnemonically fused with verbal templates in the supplementary motor cortex (Broca's centrum) when simultaneously seeing and articulating the names. The learning of new words is identical as described for behavioral templates. For example, most people who read the word *colloquialism* for the first time stumble over the syllables when pronouncing it; after a few trials, the pronunciation is fluid, indicating the consolidation of its behavioral template.

Writing is literally "reprinting" selected linguistic engrams by means of behavioral templates that are situated in area four (usually also in the left hemisphere), where activation of limb musculature and delicate movements originate. When properly motivated, linguistic engrams activate corresponding behavioral templates involved in hand and finger movements, which print our thoughts, ideas, and so forth exactly as one executes a triple somersault from a diving board.

Writing supports the earlier statement that behavioral templates cannot be visualized but are activated when we activate corresponding linguistic internal images. A concert pianist does not look at his hands in order to control their correct movements, but he internally reads his mental music sheets, whose visual engrams are, through practice, mnemonically fused with behavioral templates in the supplementary motor areas.

In summary: mind-body interactions can be conceived as the

combined result of the dual, that is, cerebral/empirical, composition of mental representations and the mnemonic fusions formed between their underlying visual, linguistic, and auditory engrams and the behavioral templates in the premotor cortex.

NOTES

1. R. F. Schmidt, ed., *Fundamentals of Neurophysiology*, trans. D. Jordan and I. Jordan (New York: Springer-Verlag, 1975).

2. O. G. Meyer and K. Roth, *Complex Movement Behaviors: The Motor-Action Controversy* (Amsterdam: Elsevier Science, 1988).

3. V. B. Mountcastle, *Handbook of Physiology: The Nervous System IV* (Bethesda, MD: American Physiological Society, 1981); G. Lynch, *Synapses, Circuits, and the Beginning of Memory* (Cambridge, MA: MIT Press, 1986).

4. C. R. Noback, N. L. Strominger, and R. J. Demarest, *The Human Nervous System*, 4th ed. (Philadelphia: Lea & Febiger, 1991).

5. M. Jeannerod, *The Cognitive Neuroscience of Action* (Oxford: Blackwell, 1997).

PART 5
PSYCHOLOGICAL AND CLINICAL IMPLICATIONS

19

FORMATION OF PERSONALITY

The term *personality* can be defined as the individual uniqueness of a person's psychological and bodily assets and the particular way in which the person utilizes them.

While the development of personality is a natural and autonomous occurrence in the existence of every human being, perusal of the literature indicates the existence of at least thirty-seven different theories of personality development.[1] Why this multitude?

There are two conceivable answers. First, the majority of theories were derived from patients' mnemonic narrations of their early life experiences collected during psychotherapy sessions. Not only are these individual narrations widely variant, they often also appeared to reflect fantasy rather than reality, as many authors have emphasized. Second, these narrations were interpreted in the absence of a common understanding of the actual nature of mental experiences. Without such understanding, it is difficult to arrive at a uniform explanation of any kind of psychological development or mental functions.

The cerebral/empirical model of the mind suggests that the development of personality involves three distinctively different yet inseparable processes:

1. The realization of one's existence as a personal entity by virtue of the empirical, dialectical self/nonself/cognition triad, whose manifestations begin to emerge during the fourth year of life and thereafter continues to be a daily recurring experience.
2. The formation and storage of visual and auditory engrams whose gestalts determine the cognitive content of the mental representations of all previous exteroceptive experiences.
3. The formation of mnemonic fusions between these engrams and the memories of the emotional or somatoceptive qualities experienced during the formation of these engrams. These mnemonic fusions convey to the cognitive content of mental representations a subjective quality and so determine the functional meaning of our psychological assets.

As detailed in chapter 11, mental representations are experienced in three categories, namely, as body images of the self, as extraneous body images of others, and as "intellectual" images representing inanimate events and objects. Nearly all mental representations are mnemonically fused with some emotional or somatoceptive quality, and most of these qualities are evoked during one's interactions with one's external world. Because no two human beings (including monozygotic twins) share the same human environment and interpersonal interactions, these interactions convey to each individual's mental representations a uniquely personal cachet and influence the ways in which each individual utilizes his or her mental and physical assets in future mental and physical activities, as conceived below.

ENVIRONMENTAL INTERACTIONS DURING THE FIRST FIVE YEARS

The majority of personality theories developed thus far have continued to employ Freud's theory that humans' early oral, anal, and oedipal experiences are the essential starting points in shaping personality. Yet none of these theories has provided an explanation of how these experiences during infancy and early childhood are permanently incorporated in the adult's personality. The apparent inability to clarify this important issue comes into a new light when we apply some of Piaget's observations during his studies of human cognitive development. Contrary to Freud's focus on emotional development, Piaget explored the origin and nature of human's intellectual development. His first reports appeared in 1920, three years before Freud advanced his final structural model of the mind without acknowledging Piaget's research. (E. Jones mentioned in his volume *The Life and Work of Sigmund Freud* that Freud paid no attention to the theories or research of psychologists.)

According to Piaget, the first twelve to eighteen months of human existence are merely sensorimotor experiences. Then follows the preoperational period heralded by the emergence of the infant's awareness of object permanence, which Piaget conceived as the first sign of some sense of cognition. However, according to the cerebral/empirical theory, the actual, that is, epistemological, sense of cognition normally does not develop before the age of four. Piaget's establishment of the emerging manifestation of abstract thinking at that age indicates that the child has come to experience internal images with a sense of selfness and with a sense of having experienced before (see chap. 3). Until that development, oral and anal experiences are strictly sensorial events and thus not mentally reproducible. This mentational absence is also incompatible with Freud's assumption that the three- to four-year-old boy entertains libidinal fantasies about the mother, like the three- to four-year-old girl presumably does about the father.

In chapter 6, I described the phenomenon of bonding and the appearance of the infant's basic trust in and attachment to his or her environment. While basic trust and attachment are generally conceived to be the products of psychological functions, they are terms used in the studies of human development to describe an infant's behavioral reactions toward an external human being only when perceiving the reappearance of a bonded object. These reactions were explained as the results of the infant's and child's formation of extraneous body images of the mother and their mnemonic fusions with the pleasurable or comforting sensory experiences evoked by the mother's feeding, diapering, or cuddling actions. If the mother's responses to the infant's signals or cries when hungry or uncomfortable are instant and consistent, bonding is a natural consequence and serves as the foundation for basic trust and attachment, which are, thus, neurophysiological phenomena. This conclusion is supported by the fact that the same phenomena are also observed between the "mother and infant" in infrahuman species and between pets and human beings.

The above thus refutes the notion that oral frustrations during early life breed "oral characters." The same is true for the notion that the "battle" between mother and infant about "anal control" causes the infant to harbor a lasting sense of shame, doubt, and frustration, all of which presumably reflect an "anal character." Shame and doubt are complex feeling states caused by mental events that are inconceivable before the age of four. Anal activities normally are natural and uneventful events and not mentally reproducible by the infant or young child. Only when the mother or other caregiver becomes frustrated and unreasonably demanding or even punitive when unable to "teach" the infant or child neatness and physical control will such disagreeable actions be stored by means of the child's extraneous body images of the mother's actions. Their association(s) with unpleasant if not fearful experiences are bound to interfere with the development of basic trust and attachment or negatively affect previously established ones. Furthermore, it is very likely that parents' attitudes to toilet training are but one indication of their general love and care for their offspring.

Besides the significance of the qualitative aspects of environmental interactions, the quantity of their occurrences is equally important, particularly during the first year. As detailed in chapter 6, the brain of the human infant contains at birth a modest amount of nonactive neurons and neural pathways. During the first six months, metabolic activities unfold in a predictable sequence from the occipital lobes to the frontal lobes, hand in hand with specific brain activities. At the end of the first year, neurons have multiplied into the millions. However, these developments only take place in a stimulus-rich environment. Numerous studies compiled in *The Competent Infant* by L. J. Stone, H. T. Smith, and L. B. Murphy have established that when an infant is deprived during the first twelve months of life of ample environmentally induced perceptual and sensorial experiences, the brain fails to unfold its innate potential of neuronal and neural growth.[2] The irreversible consequences are stunted mental development; the incapability of anticipating the emotional or somatoceptive consequences of the mother's reappearances; failure of the phenomena of bonding, basic trust, and attachment to develop; and failure of the motivation to look forward to reappearing objects to develop, which impedes future social behavior.

To demonstrate the seriousness of the lack of environmental interactions during early development, H. F. Harlow replaced mothers of newborn monkeys with a "surrogate" mother made of an iron frame covered with a furry coat, with a bottle filled with milk tied to the "chest." Every monkey so "raised" failed to thrive and became reclusive, avoiding all contact with other, naturally raised monkeys.

I already mentioned Spitz's observations of normally cared-for infants who (for various reasons) had to be placed in an orphanage at the age of six months. Even though these infants were properly and timely fed and diapered, they cried frequently, showed no appetite, and lost weight, all signs of a depressed state, which Spitz described as "anaclitic" (i.e., psychologically dependent) depression, supporting the significance of the formation of attachment and its continuous reinforcement. Follow-up of these infants as adults twenty, thirty, and forty years later showed in all of them a lower-than-average IQ, restricted social interactions, and various forms of psychopathology.

Another example of the environmental impact on personality development is the adverse affects of parents' differential treatment of and attitudes toward their children. When a three- to four-year-old child, while developing his or her cognitive abilities, observes that he or she is being loved less than siblings are, is often singled out to carry out unpleasant chores, never seems to be able to please parents, or, most painful of all, is frequently ignored, such experiences have a devastating impact on the growing child's notion of self-worth. There is in the literature no better illustration of the opposite consequences of a warm, supportive, encouraging, and loving environment versus a loveless, nonforgiving, and demanding milieu than E. H. Erikson's formulations of the nature of identity at each milestone of psychological development.[3]

ENVIRONMENTAL INTERACTIONS FROM FIVE TO TWENTY-FIVE YEARS

A complete change in the nature, intensity, and consequences of the interactions between the growing child (now in possession of a sense of self, nonself, and cognition) and the external world takes place in three subsequent phases: the elementary school years from ages six to twelve; adolescence, from twelve to eighteen; and pre-adulthood from nineteen to twenty-five. The details of these interactions and their consequences have been discussed in chapters 13–15 and therefore are only highlighted here.

All our experiences are crystallized in the forms of body images of the self, extraneous body images of others, and intellectual images, all mnemonically fused with the memories of a given pleasurable or displeasurable emotional and somatoceptive experience. Eventually, the normally developed adult possesses "a" mind that is composed of a self-concept that includes the bodily self and the psychological self, which consists of a mosaic of images of people (parents, siblings, relatives, and friends) and a collection of environmental rules (the constituents of "the" superego) that determine how he utilizes his mental representations when interacting with others.

These environmental rules usually lead to adaptations of certain behaviors if they should cause adverse environmental reactions or tarnish one's integrity or self-worth. Consistent with the views on mind-body interactions presented in the previous chapter, the need for and selection of behavioral modifications in social intercourse are one's judgments of how one is received by others. This is contrary to Freud's theory of adaptation. Freud conceptualized that humans develop defense mechanisms to cope with conflicts between the superego and the id and that defense mechanisms are unconsciously developed by the ego. There are two problems with that concept. First, how is one to explain the ego's construction of unconscious mechanisms? By which process do these mechanisms unconsciously fulfill their (assumed) tasks of forgetting, displacement, reaction formation, and such?

As detailed in chapter 11, ego activities cannot be considered unconscious because the ego is a component of the inextricable triad of the self, nonself, and cognition. Furthermore, self-protective defense maneuvers can be conceived as the products of the innate, thus natural, functions of the limbic system, that is, the amygdaloid nuclei that induce the prefrontal cortex to repress inappropriate motor activities, memories, thoughts, and so forth. When a given thought, memory, or action is experienced with an unbearable emotion, the amygdaloid nuclei may inhibit the actualization of the involved visual engram and so represses the realization of questionable mental content. The same rationale explains how the amygdaloid nuclei prevent the activation of a given behavioral template if associated with intolerable emotions or socially unacceptable pleasurable qualities.

Besides these biologically induced defenses, most humans deliberately thus consciously utilize in everyday life a wide variety of activities to mask certain feelings—guilt, embarrassment—or to please others, as illustrated in the discussion on the human encounter (see chap. 17). We may thus distinguish two categories of defense mechanisms: Freud's "unconscious" repression as the result of a biological (as Freud predicted) process to avoid *internal* turmoil and a set of voluntary behavior patterns or inhibitions aimed at the establishment and preservation of amiable and productive social and interpersonal relationships. If effective, any of such behaviors eventually become, by repetitive use, incorporated in one's repertoire of body images and thus provide another example of the environmental influence on personality characteristics.

CEREBRAL ENDOWMENTS

As much as the psychological and economic fortunes of human infants are determined by their environment, so are they the willy-nilly recipients of the inherited qualities of their brains at birth. All regions and neural pathways may be in place at birth, but their functional potentials differ from one newborn to another and greatly contribute to the individual uniqueness of behavioral and mental development. Even parents without psychological expertise have no difficulty concluding in a matter of weeks that their latest newborn is far more alert and socially responsive than any of the siblings among whom the parents also observed such differences between an "early walker" at ten months while the other "waited" for eighteen months. One sibling was a peaceful sleeper and showed a pleasant disposition while awake; the other was a restless sleeper and "cranky" when up and about.

It now is possible to trace certain behavioral characteristics back to specific areas and functions of the brain that also contribute to the uniqueness of personality. The ability to form, store, and retrieve memories is a function of the left and right memory banks and are distinctively different from person to person. The rapidity of speech and general motility reflects the innate qualities of the limbic system, such as social responsiveness, gregariousness, and a bubbly personality versus an aloof, phlegmatic individual known as an introvert as opposed to an extrovert. Therefore, the distinction between congenital and developmentally acquired behavioral and mental characteristics by way of a thorough anamnesis is an important process in the determination of the appropriate therapy for personality disorders.

NOTES

1. C. S. Hall and G. Lindzey, *Theories of Personality* (New York: Wiley, 1978); A. Burton, *Operational Theories of Personality* (New York: Brunner/Matzel, 1974); J. Aronoff, A. I. Rabin, and R. A. Zucker, *The Emergence of Personality* (New York: Springer, 1987).

2. L. J. Stone, H. T. Smith, and L. B. Murphy, *The Competent Infant* (New York: Basic Books, 1973).

3. E. H. Erikson, "Identity and the Life Cycle," *Psychological Issues* 1 (1963): 101–72.

20

PSYCHOPATHOLOGY

Of all the mental concepts advanced during the last century, the one most affected by the persistent difficulties in clarifying the origin and nature of the mind is that of *psychopathology*. The term is generally defined as the manifestations of mental disorders or the study of mental disorders. But how can one identify mental pathology without a clear definition of the nature and function of the normal mind? As discussed in chapter 11, Freud had recognized this and conceived three hypothetical structures (id, ego, and superego) whose internal psychodynamics presumably may lead to pathological interactions or conditions. Yet the actual existence or occurrence of such mental structures has never been established.

According to the cerebral/empirical concept of the mind, mental experiences are not functions of the mind but independently originating cognitive units (mental representations) that serve as the constituents of the mind. Each mental representation consists of two components: a cognitive content (a visual gestalt determined by an actualized visual engram) and an emotional or somatoceptive quality determined by mnemonically fused somatoceptive or emotional memories. The pleasurable or displeasurable quality of these memories determine whether a given mental event may be actualized or repressed by virtue of the prefrontal cortex.

Because mental experiences are the combinative products of cerebral events and their mnemonically fused emotional and somatoceptive qualities, abnormal mental experiences are, then, either symptomatic of improperly actualized mental representations, or the reflections of associated disagreeable emotional or somatoceptive memories, both capable of interfering with an efficient utilization of mental representations. We may, thus, distinguish two categories of psychopathology, namely, cerebral versus psychodynamic psychopathology. This distinction is consistent with the traditional concepts of organic versus nonorganic psychopathology. To illustrate how the cerebral/empirical concept of mental experiences enables us to conceive pathological mental conditions, I discuss three different forms of psychopathology, Alzheimer's dementia, the frontal lobe disorder, and bipolar disorder, followed by a speculative discussion of schizophrenia.

DEMENTIAS

Dementias are caused by defective cerebral structures. This was the conclusion of the German pathologist A. Alzheimer, who introduced in 1907 the term *presenile dementia* to refer to the occurrence of mental deterioration in adults between fifty and sixty years of age.[1] His anatomical and neurohistological investigations revealed the presence of neuritic plaques and neurofibrillary tangles mostly in the hippocampal areas (the relay stations between our memory banks and the limbic system). Brain imaging studies have shown that the earliest manifestations of mental deterioration coincide with cerebral abnormalities in the parietal regions (where our visual and auditory memory banks are located).[2]

In 1970, the Swedish researcher B. E. Tomlinsen et al. also reported a linear correlation between the severity of "involutional" (i.e., age-related or senescent) dementia and the number of neurofibrillary strangles and neuritic plaques in the brain and thus identified the common cerebral pathology in presenile (Alzheimer's) dementia and the one related to senescence.[3]

The symptomatology of dementias is clearly established as are their correlations with specific MRI findings, which make it possible to translate all findings into the psychopathology of dementias in terms of the cerebral/empirical model of the mind. The inability to remember recent events, physical activities, or changes in surroundings and/or the dissolution of established memories indicate a faltering capacity to form new engrams. The manifestations of forgetfulness and difficulty with retrieving names of humans or inanimate objects and events reflect in addition to a reduced excitability of visual, linguistic, and auditory engrams an impaired conductivity in the neural pathways that underlie the mnemonic fusions between left and right hemispheres (the stations for visual, i.e., object engrams, and linguistic, i.e., word engrams).

Deficiencies in recognizing familiar objects or people during spontaneous remembering and in carrying on a fluent and intelligible conversation also reflect the erosion of visual, auditory, and linguistic engrams. This erosion follows a characteristic pattern: Recent memory is lost first, remote memory gradually shrinks to engrams formed during earlier life, indicating a retrograde decay of chronologically stored engrams (and confirming the notion of the chronological storage of visual and auditory memories in sequence of their occurrence, as proposed in chapter 3). Hypometabolism in the frontal cortex explains its withering capacity to selectively inactivate redundant or irrelevant visual engrams and behavioral templates.[4] Thoughts and memories are perseverative and become incoherent; verbal and behavioral expressions are unrestrained, resulting in a loss of decorum, abstract thinking, and the utilization of bizarre motor activities.

The affected limbic system not only accounts for the changes in endocrine functions, biological rhythms, and sleeping pattern, it is also responsible for the disappearance of affective expressivity and recognition of the affective expressions of others (usually referred to as "aprosody").[5]

The continuous disappearance of engrams eventually makes differentiation between images and percepts impossible, so that the dialectical self/nonself/cognition triad is no longer experienced.

Fragmented memories are now experienced as actual happenings, and the individual appears to be hallucinating. The awareness of object permanence dissipates, leaving the individual at the stage of where his or her empirical mind once started: the noncognitive state of infancy.

J. S. Maxmen correctly emphasized "the unusual role of etiology in mental disorders. Psychiatry is the only medical specialty which treats diseases without known etiology."[6] Hence the continual efforts in the following discussions to at least conceive some etiological origin where none is yet known.

Because there is a linear correlation between the extent of dementia and the number of neurofibrillary filaments,[7] the etiology of Alzheimer's disease must be sought in the decay of neurons and neural pathways in senile plaques and neurofibrillary tangles. These neural and neuronal abnormalities take us back to Edelman's invaluable discovery of N-CAM molecules (see chap. 7), whose function is to connect selected groups of cells into permanent configurations such as visual, auditory, or linguistic engrams. *The appearance of senile plaques and neurofibrillary tangles suggests a failure of N-CAMs to form and sustain proper connections between the neurons in the memory banks.*

Another critical change is the dissolution of the extensive neural networks that combine cognitive content with subjective meanings by virtue of mnemonic fusions. Mnemonic fusions are formed by synaptic processes. Not only are mnemonic fusions no longer formed (lack of synopsin?), but established mnemonic fusions are lost as well.

FRONTAL LOBE DISORDER

As detailed in chapter 10, the prefrontal cortex is not the seat of intellectual functions, as has long been assumed, but serves as a regulatory mediator that operates by way of inhibiting irrelevant or inappropriate thoughts, memories, or physical or verbal motor actions and thus promote efficient and appropriate intellectual, emotional, and behavioral activities. This regulatory function is monitored by the amygdaloid nuclei in the limbic system.

This supervisory function may become impaired by head trauma, cerebral tumors, toxic states, or infections such as the *Treponema pallidum*, which caused classical forebrain syndromes during the first half of the last century, before the availability of treatment. Prefrontal psychopathology is marked by the inability to effectively and adaptively exercise one's intellectual, emotional, and physical actions. Recent investigations have shown the occurrence of defective inhibitions of singular intellectual or behavioral functions such as Williams syndrome (a genetic form of mental retardation and characteristic physical abnormalities), ADHD, and obsessive-compulsive disorder. These studies have conclusively demonstrated a dysfunctional frontal lobe in these conditions.[8]

BIPOLAR DISORDER

The "manic-depressive" disorder is a functional disorder and, as conceived below, cerebral in origin. Its psychopathology and periodic occurrences reflect *quantitative extremes* rather than *structural changes*. During the manic states, all mental and motor activities are accelerated, and emotions are jubilant. The mind races; verbal and physical activities reflect boundless energy. Depressive episodes are characterized by profound physical, intellectual, and social underactivity; and melancholic spirits accompanied by lack of motivation. During normal periods, all systems are usually functioning efficiently, indicating the absence of a permanent defect.

The origin of these bipolar oscillations has remained elusive. Most investigations have concentrated on the role of catecholamines, but reported increases and decreases of these neurotransmitters are more likely to be reflections of mental overactivities and underactivities rather than their causes. According to the cerebral/empirical theory of the mind, all mental and physical activities originate as cerebral activities, and these cerebral activities are initiated by the various centers of the limbic system (see chap. 10), implicating this system as a likely source of the abnormal mental and physical activities in bipolar subjects.

This possibility is suggested by laboratory studies of electrical stimulation of its different centers. Stimulation of the septal region creates a purring, well-spirited cat, while ablation of this region results in a "depressed," that is, totally withdrawn and immobile, animal that no longer feeds and grooms itself. Loss of septal region activities in humans results in the loss of energy and lack of libido, motivation, and social interactions. These symptoms responded to Heath's implantation of a "cerebral pacemaker" in the septal region of depressed individuals who did not respond to conventional therapies.

It further is important to note that both manic and depressive episodes are not limited to abnormal mental and physical activities but include the gamut of limbic functions. Bipolar patients show during both manic and depressive episodes a hormonal imbalance[9] and disruption in diurnal vegetative and sleep rhythms (insomnia or dawning insomnia).

What might cause the limbic system to periodically accelerate or decelerate its stimulation of other brain regions? All of the above suggest the involvement of the suprachiasmatic nucleus (SCN), which is situated in the anterior portion of the hypothalamus. The SCN is a circadian pacemaker, that is, a *self-sustained biological oscillator*.[10] Bilateral ablation of the SCN results in the abolishment of circadian rhythms. Another component in the circadian system is the pineal gland, which in nearly all vertebrates rhythmically produces the hormone melatonin by converting serotonin under control of the SCN. Interactions with other pacemakers still are under investigation.

The role of the SCN in circadian rhythms became clear in 1972 following the discovery of the *retino-hypothalamic tract*. This tract is a nonvisual retinal pathway and is responsible for entrainment (the synchronization of circadian pacemakers to environmental cycles). The SCN, in turn, has a crucial role in the generation of circadian rhythms of most behavioral and physiological phenomena, as demonstrated by SCN lesion studies in a variety of species, including primates.[11]

The above suggests how the limbic system serves as the "electrical power house" for mental activities as proposed in chapter 11: when stimulated, its electrical potentials are transmitted by means of neurotransmitters to various brain centers, including the memory banks and their visual and auditory engrams. In the absence of any other explanation for the drastic disturbance in the circadian rhythms of bipolar individuals, it appears reasonable to consider a temporary defect in either the retinohypothalamic pathway or in the SCN. A temporary defect in the SCN would be consistent with the notion that *periodic diseases are diseases of regulation*, as suggested by C. van der Velde and M. W. Gordon.[12] This notion may also explain the benefits of phototherapy in seasonal affective disorder.

SCHIZOPHRENIA

Schizophrenia is psychiatry's most unpredictable disorder in its course, its symptomatology, and physical or biological concomitants. The only consistent feature of this illness has been the elusiveness of its pathophysiology and etiology.

When the German psychiatrist Emil Kraepelin identified in 1898 the symptomatology of what is presently referred to as schizophrenia, he coined the term *dementia praecox* to imply that the "mental deterioration" of afflicted patients was caused by an endogenous, that is, cerebral, factor. In 1911 (four years after Alzheimer had published his discovery of presenile dementia and its underlying cerebral pathology), the Swiss psychiatrist Eugen Bleuler discarded the idea of mental deterioration and suggested to replace the term *dementia praecox* with the term *schizophrenia* to depict the characteristic feature of the disease: the dissociation between mental functions. He further suggested that the bizarreness of schizophrenic symptoms was the result of Freudian repression.

Following these formulations, numerous efforts to clarify a cerebral cause of schizophrenic symptoms have been undertaken, yet no definitive neuronal, neurochemical, or neurophysiological abnormality has been detected thus far.

While this absence supported Bleuler's view of schizophrenia as a psychological disorder, matters changed in favor of Kraepelin's cerebral concept at the end of the twentieth century, when brain imaging technologies became available. Within two decades, the results of all MRI, PET, and SPECT studies led to the unanimous agreement among researchers around the world that the brain in schizophrenia is reduced in overall size; ventricles are enlarged; and there is cortical wasting and volume decrease in most limbic structures, all thoroughly discussed by Arnold and R. C. Gur.[12]

MRI technology also made it possible to gauge the blood flow in separate brain areas and so correlate abnormal activities in specific brain regions with specific schizophrenic symptoms. Four such areas have been identified:

1. *Frontal lobes.* Weinberger et al. established that schizophrenic subjects while performing abstract tasks do not show an increase in blood flow in the prefrontal cortex as normal subjects do, yet show a fair capacity of memory.[14] They suggested that hypofrontality might have a causative role in the impairment of the schizophrenic's thought processes and erratic behaviors, as seen in frontal lobe disorders.

2. *Temporal lobes.* A. J. Saykin et al. observed that their schizophrenic subjects are impaired in both abstract ability and in memory and learning, although more so in the latter two functions.[15] They associated these findings with a "selective temporal lobe deficit," that is, the combined dysfunctions of the medial temporal region, hippocampus, and amygdaloid nuclei, which are all involved in learning and memory. Furthermore, dysfunctions in the left hemisphere were associated with poverty of thought, illogical thinking, and auditory hallucinations.

3. *Basal ganglia.* The caudate, putamen, and global pallidus, which are, directly and indirectly (via the thalamus), neurally connected with the frontal lobes, show a slight but consistent increase in activity during MRI studies with schizophrenic patients. However, these findings were observed only in schizophrenic individuals who had been treated with neuroleptic medications, which may account for these observations.

4. *The limbic system.* A. C. Lahti et al. established[15] that the

administration of ketamine (which exacerbates positive symptoms in schizophrenic individuals) caused an increase in blood flow in the anterior cingulate area but a decrease in the hippocampus and the lingual gyrus.[16]

Since the above correlations between given brain regions and given schizophrenic symptoms have now been known for two decades, the question arises: Why haven't they made it possible to understand the pathophysiology of schizophrenia?

This problem can be attributed to the traditional use of the term *mental symptoms* in the absence of a definition of the mind or mental functions. If the cerebral/empirical theory of the mind is a valid concept, then cognition, memory, and any other mental experience, normal or pathological, are empirical epiphenomena, not functions of a specific brain activity, as little as they are functions of the mind because they serve as its constituents (see chap. 4). Although mental experiences originate as cerebral events (i.e., as actualized visual engrams), these become mental events only when experienced with the dialectical sense of having experienced before by virtue of our simultaneous experiences of actual visual percepts.

Therefore, if the schizophrenic's mental symptoms are indeed the products of abnormal cerebral activities, only a comparative examination of the schizophrenic's mental aberrations with normal mental experiences and their underlying cerebral activities might enable us to understand the cerebral psychopathology of schizophrenia. For this comparison, I use six categories of symptoms that are generally considered as pathognomonic of schizophrenia, and interpret their deviations from normal mental functions in terms of cerebral/empirical principles.

1. *Disordered thought processes.* The poverty of thought, the looseness of associations, word salad, thought blockage, thought withdrawal, and paraphrasing all indicate interruptions of the normal flow of thoughts. The experience of the normal mind is characterized by a continual flow of thoughts. This continuity suggests that we continually experience actualized

visual engrams during the waking states. While we are able to direct our train of thought, we cannot "turn off" our thinking at any time. This indicates that our visual engrams are actualized by some independent cerebral source. As detailed in chapter 10, the only conceivable part of the brain that is capable of autonomously actualizing visual engrams is the limbic system. Via the reciprocal neural pathways between the hippocampus and the visual and auditory engrams in our memory banks in the parietal lobes, these engrams are mnemonically fused with the mnemonic centers for pain, pleasure, and displeasure in the parahippocampus, hypothalamic regions, amygdaloid nuclei, and the anterior and posterior cingulate cortex. Activation of these limbic areas may arouse the actualization of associated visual or auditory engrams. Most limbic areas derive their stimulative power from the SCN, as discussed in the previous section. The above implies that the interruption of thoughts in schizophrenia may reflect a defect in any limbic center, a defect in the hippocampus, or irregularities in the SCN.

2. *Delusional and concrete thinking.* Delusions in schizophrenia reflect a patient's faulty description of a given cognitive content. Their usual persistence suggests permanently formed mnemonic fusions between given visual engrams and unrelated linguistic engrams. Concrete thinking reflects the lack of conceptual thinking. Under normal mental conditions, conceptual thinking involves the assembling by means of linguistic engrams various visual engrams that have a given subjective quality or related cognitive content in common into a verbal representative. This sorting process requires the capacity to internally compare and include related mental representations while excluding unrelated ones. This sorting activity is a function of the prefrontal cortex. Therefore, the schizophrenic's delusional descriptions of ideas, concrete thoughts, or "woolly" concepts indicate a failure of the prefrontal cortex in suppressing irrelevant thoughts and ideas. This failure is apparent in all other functions, as shown momentarily.

3. *Abnormal affective experiences.* Schizophrenic individuals commonly show flatness of affect, lack of motivation, and no
interest in their environment. Under normal conditions,
humans' emotional states and their motivational stimulation
for action and interaction originate in the septal region. Lack
of affectivity in schizophrenia reflects either a malfunctioning
septal region or reduced stimulation by the SCN. Inappropriate expressivity reflects mnemonic fusions between mental
representations and unrelated emotional memories. The
absence of emotional rapport during interpersonal interactions (experienced by others as "praecox feelings") indicates
a lack of emotional arousal by extraneous body images when
meeting others, suggesting the possibility of malfunctioning
neural pathways.
4. *Hallucinations.* Many schizophrenics experience sensorial
events in the absence of external stimuli. This suggests several
causes, including: abnormal activations in primary perceptual brain regions (unlikely) or actualized visual or auditory
engrams experienced as actual percepts due to lack of experiencing the self/nonself/cognition triad in the absence of
simultaneous experiences of engrams and actual visual percepts. Reduced or interrupted external perceptions may reflect
an RAS defect caused by a dysfunctional SCN. This faltering
triad also explains the phenomenon of *Gedanken lautwerden*
(thoughts becoming loud).
5. *Bizarre motor activities.* Mannerisms, posturing, catatonia, and
echolalia reflect randomly activated behavioral templates in
the premotor cortex or Broca by the indiscriminate limbic
system combined with a dysfunctional prefrontal cortex.
6. *Attention deficits.* Both Kraepelin and Bleuler considered lack
of attention a characteristic "symptom" of schizophrenia.
This symptom is in and of itself a clear manifestation of a
dysfunctional RAS and SCN.[17]

While the above indicates that the two brain regions involved in
the psychopathology of schizophrenia are the limbic structures and

the prefrontal cortex, the dysfunction of the latter in schizophrenia is not necessarily a defect of the prefrontal cortex per se. Its inhibitory function is directed by the amygdaloid nuclei, which are not only integral parts of the limbic system, but also the most critical elements in the preservation of our physical, mental, and emotional well-being. This suggests that the limbic system, if not just the amygdala, might be the sole cause of schizophrenic symptomatology.

This suggestion is entirely consistent with the neuropathological findings of postmortem studies of the limbic structures (entorhinal cortex, hippocampi, cingulate cortex, anterior thalamus) of the schizophrenic brain. E. Falke and B. Bogerts reported reduced number of cells; D. V. Jeste and J. B. Lohr found abnormalities in cell size; A. B. Scheibel and J. Kovelman observed neuronal disorganization; N. Colter et al. noticed abnormal shape and cell structure; S. E. Arnold et al. observed abnormal cellular organization in layer-2 neurons.[18] Furthermore, MRI studies by Tamminga et al. disclosed functional deficits throughout the limbic system.[19]

Failure of the limbic system and its amygdaloids explains the underactivity of the prefrontal cortex, its hypometabolism, and the reduced concentration of gamma-aminobutyric acid (GABA) in the prefrontal cortex. It also explains the simultaneous occurrence of positive and negative symptoms. Negative symptoms presumably occur because of a lack of septal region activity, while positive symptoms such as hallucinations or delusions result from a lack of prefrontal cortex repression.

What might be the cause of these pathological changes in the limbic system? Although schizophrenia clearly reflects a genetic disposition, the mechanism of transmission is obscure. It may be of importance that the first manifestations of schizophrenia usually appear between the ages of fifteen and twenty-five and that some schizophrenic patients show a surprising improvement from age fifty onward. These observations raise the question whether increased and reduced activities of certain hormones during adolescence and the menopausal stage may be instrumental in the precipitation and disappearance of the manifestation of schizophrenia because of their intense interactions with various limbic structures.

Another cerebral area in the limbic system of interest in the search for etiology is the SCN because of its role as the principal provider of "mental energy" (see chap. 19). While there are no indications of disturbed circadian rhythms in schizophrenic individuals, it is conceivable that a reduced input of photoelectrical impulses might play a role in the functional deficits of the various limbic areas cited above. As discussed, the SCN receives its energy from the retina via the retino-hypothalamic (nonvisual) pathway. This retinal source of photoelectric power brings back to mind the abnormal ophthalmologic findings in schizophrenia during the seventies, namely, pupillary constrictions and saccadic eye movements. These findings have been widely examined but failed to produce any connection with the schizophrenic process. The fact that these abnormalities were observed in only 60 percent of the patients studied should not have discouraged further research in view of the symptomatic variability in schizophrenia. A ten-year follow-up of one hundred hospitalized chronic schizophrenics by van der Velde showed during those ten years (1965–1975) a remarkable individual variability in symptoms and subsequent changes in diagnostic categories, different responses to the same medications, unusual changes in weight, and acute exacerbations superimposed on chronic symptomatology.[20] Such individual variability is not apparent from cross-sectional studies; only longitudinal studies will reveal that a given symptom or therapeutic response is absent during one episode but present during the next periodic exacerbation.

A few comments are in order with regard to the suggestion that both bipolar disorder and schizophrenia may be considered limbic disorders. The manic-depressive disease is a *quantitative* disorder, namely, a periodic change in given psychological functions that in and of themselves are not abnormal but show abnormal changes in "volume." The manic patient is euphoric and hyperactive, shows pressure of speech, feels on top of the world, and has grandiose ideas about his wealth and intellectual capabilities. Depressive episodes are marked by melancholia, lack of energy, lack of communication and initiative, self-accusations, and often suicidal ideation. Thus, both reflect a change in mental and physical energy, but mental contents and activities always are in line with the emotional state. These periodic oscillations may reflect dysfunctions of the SCN.

The symptoms of schizophrenia are incomprehensibly discongruent, reflecting permanent functional deficits of the entire limbic that affect all other cerebral functions.

PSYCHODYNAMIC PSYCHOPATHOLOGY

Most theories on psychodynamic psychopathology are based on Freud's concepts of the structural (ego/superego/id) model of the mind, the existence of the unconscious, and the formation of psychological defense mechanisms in response to intrapsychic conflicts. Freud postulated that such conflicts arise between sexual or aggressive id impulses and one's conscience (the superego). The consequent experience of fear or guilt induces the ego to produce unconscious defense mechanisms that "move" painful or unwanted ideas, memories, or drives into the id, where they remain active as "unconscious mental processes." These processes are presumed to be responsible for the development of psychopathological states or personality disorders.

The problem with these formulations is that they were developed while the exact nature of the mind had yet to be clarified. The implications of this problem were brought to light in chapter 11 when I compared Freud's concepts with the cerebral/empirical theory of the mind. This comparison led to the following conclusions, which I highlight for the reader's convenience.

1. Since all mental experiences are the empirical results of the *inextricable self/nonself/cognition triad*, whose occurrence is contingent upon our simultaneous experiences of the dialectical opposites of internal images and visual percepts, the concept of *unconscious mental processes* appears to be an untenable idea.

2. The phenomenon of *unconscious memory* can be explained by means of a natural process. For example, most humans expe-

rience at one time or another the inability to retrieve a given memory, name, or idea while knowing that they know it. Freud considered this "forgetting" to be the result of a psychological defense mechanism that he named *repression*, unconsciously produced for the purpose of eliminating the experience of distressing feelings associated with that particular memory. However, this mnemonic repression can be explained as the consequence of the *neurophysiological inhibitory function of the prefrontal cortex*, as detailed in chapter 10. This function is induced by the amygdaloid nuclei whenever we experience anxiety, guilt, or anger associated with a given mental representation, causing the inactivation of a visual or auditory engram by means of the reciprocal neural pathways between the prefrontal cortex and the visual and auditory memory banks. The consequent prevention of the actualization of a given mental representation thus "keeps" undesirable wishes, ideas, or memories unconscious, that is, out of awareness.

3. While Freud's notion of intrapsychic conflicts was based on the hypothetical existence of mental *structures*, it can be argued that human's psychological difficulties originate from identifiably occurring *interpersonal conflicts*. Because our notions of self and cognition (*Eigenwelt*) are inextricably experienced with our sense of nonself (*Umwelt*), we inevitably and constantly are aware of the reactions and opinions of others to and about our appearances and actions, physical, mental, or verbal. Their opinions and reactions are contained in our extraneous body images, which are the constituents of our concept of the superego (see chap. 11). These images are mnemonically fused with the emotional qualities that were simultaneously experienced during our interactions with others and also are mnemonically fused with our own body images. Environmental appraisals and disapprovals not only determine during the developmental years the kind of person the growing individual is and what his or her shortcomings are, they also define which behaviors are acceptable

or not, which should be adapted or eliminated, and which actions promote desirable interpersonal relationships.

Our own body images thus enable us to predict the desirable or undesirable consequences of our bodily actions and so provide us with a repertoire of gestures and motions from which we select the appropriate behaviors that promote proper interpersonal relationships. For instance, when meeting a disliked relative or an authoritarian individual, we may produce a conspicuously bright and kind smile to "cover up" our negative or hostile feelings. While Freud considered this "reaction formation" as an unconscious ego defense mechanism that "transforms" an unacceptable, aggressive id impulse into an opposite action, he never elucidated how one unconsciously manages such complicated mind-body interactions. It can be argued that the above example of reaction formation is a reflection of making effective use of the biopsychosocial fabric (engrams/cognition/self-representation) of our mental representations to prevent interpersonal conflict.

The cerebral/empirical model suggests that there are two modes of mental defenses: (1) the autonomously operating biological function of the prefrontal cortex, which serves the preservation of life in all species by virtue of specific devices (such as the chameleon's capacity to change skin colors), and (2) mentally designed changes or inhibitions of selected verbal or bodily actions based on the social or interpersonal consequences, as indicated by our mental representations, that is, our body images and extraneous body images of others.

Thus, while Freud emphasized the internal nature of conflicts between id, ego, and superego, the dialectical/empirical interpretation of our psychological existence emphasizes that most psychological conflicts arise from our interpersonal and social interactions, which determine our choice of psychological coping behaviors. Most defense mechanisms become "second nature" by repeated use (if effective) and contribute to the characteristics of personality that be may be favorable or pathological and result in a personality disorder that is thus often a product of the environment. Maxmen's overview of personality disorders clearly indicate that the origin and nature of most personality disorders can be traced back to the early years of development.

SOMATOFORM MENTAL DISORDERS

While schizophrenia is psychiatry's most vexing problem, somato-form disorders affect all medical specialties, with a much higher incidence and equally puzzling dynamics. There is no agreement among researchers on how to use the ambiguous definitions of the *DSM–IV* distinctions between somatoform disorders such as soma-tization, conversion disorder, chronic pain disorder, or hypochon-driasis. Nor are there any controlled studies to suggest an effective psychological or behavioral therapy or to reveal how mental events may cause bodily symptoms.

A major problem is the unchallenged assumption that if the occurrence of bodily symptoms cannot be explained by organic fac-tors, they must be of psychic origin. For example, the term *psychoso-matic disorders, sensu stricto*, suggests interactions between mind and body and thus should be eligible to the cerebral/empirical interpre-tations, as discussed in chapter 18 on mind-body interactions. How-ever, psychosomatic disorders as classified today mainly involve abnormal occurrences of the *autonomous nervous system* and thus do not involve visually perceptible parts of the body as an object. Fur-thermore, the condition of hypochondriasis does not involve actual neurophysiological or bodily experiences. It is a phobic disorder with physical health or illness as targets, like the bacteria-phobic individual who avoids touching doorknobs or dirty towels without worrying about doors or towels per se.

The term *psychosomatic* was introduced by Johann Christian Heinroth in 1818 to refer to insomnia as an "emotional/bodily" problem. However, during the last century, the accent has shifted predominantly to physical symptoms that reflect the autonomous nervous system and neurophysiological functions.

Several theories have suggested that somatization may represent a defense mechanism to cope with an unresolved intrapsychic conflict. Besides the question of the unexplained transformation of a mental (nonmaterial) problem into a physical one, it also seems a rather paradoxical way of "coping" with an intrapsychic problem by creating a physical one.

The only conceivable psychosomatic, that is, mind-body, disorder is the *conversion disorder*. Freud introduced this term in 1920 to explain "the mysterious leap from the mental to the physical." He conceived this leap to be a conversion from a mental conflict into a physical disorder as he did, for example, in Anne O's case of paralysis. The cerebral/empirical model suggests the following explanation of such "conversion":

> A 49-year-old woman was hospitalized at a long-term-care facility for chronic neurological diseases, for a bilateral paralysis of both legs of three month duration suggestive of amyotrophic lateral sclerosis. Because of the patient's conspicuous lack of concern (*la belle indifference*) psychiatric consultation was requested. The consultation prompted a hypnotic session during which the patient appeared to be able to move both legs. Subsequent sessions revealed that the paralysis had developed suddenly one week after she had been raped. She had kept this incident secret from her "good and caring but very fastidious" husband out of fear that she would "lose him."[21]

Rather than viewing this paralysis as a symbolic *conversion* of unbearable guilt, one might conceive it as the consequence of a defensive function of the amygdaloids instructing the prefrontal cortex to repress the unbearable memory of the body image of the legs (associated with the rape), as well as the corresponding behavioral templates in the motor cortex. The inability to recognize her own legs because of their blocked body images would explain the phenomenon of *la belle indifference* not as the consequence of a psychological conversion but as the inability to "feel" the existence of her legs caused by a biological suppression. The patient successfully responded to psychotherapy.

Since no specific mental problems have ever been associated

with somatization disorders (besides the frequent accompaniment of a depressive state), how then can we conceive their development? B. Kellner concluded his book *Psychosomatic Syndromes and Somatic Symptoms* with the following passage: "no single theory such as defense mechanisms, a conflict resolution, a method of symbolic communication, or reinforcement by gain can explain the various phenomena of somatization."[22]

There is considerable agreement that the occurrence of somatization disorders is somehow linked to *stress*. The role of stress has been implicated in the many theories on psychosomatics and has been detailed in H. I. Kaplan's comprehensive review in the CPT. H. Selye considered the occurrence of stress paramount to the "conditioning" with somatic experiences. Reiser suggested that hormonal activities released by stress situations act back on the brain as a target so that preprogrammed but dormant circuits are activated, including visceral functions.[23] Reiser further theorized the existence of predisposing factors (such as visceral organ specificity), although some of them may be derived from past psychological experiences.

The main problem with stress theories is the meaning of the term *stress*, which has never been successfully defined. Stress is not a specific function of a specific limbic center. It is conceived here as an emotional by-product of an individual's realization of being besieged by extraneous conditions that deprive the individual of his or her capacity to his or her physical or psychological existence and are beyond control. Stress situations can produce mixtures of anger, bitterness, sadness, hopelessness, helplessness. Stress can be caused by numerous events: an endogenous depression, financial concerns, loss of employment, or a meaningful interpersonal relationship.

Since there is no identifiable limbic area to explain the origin of stress, we might conceive stress as an empirical sensation superimposed upon unpleasant emotions whose origin can be localized (amygdala, hypothalamus). The latter are mnemonically fused with both secondary somatoceptive areas. A threatened monkey or cat claws because the innate connection between amygdaloids and area forty-four. So are the asthmatic patients consistent in response to the sight of an unpleasant object. Because of the existence of mnemonic fusions, the very thought of an unpleasant situation or relationship may explain the occurrence of urticaria, hyperacidity, or pruritis, all consistently indicating synaptic connections and reciprocal ones.

Another mysterious physical condition is *anorexia nervosa*. Considering the periodicity of its manifestations and, thus, the possibility of some regulatory defect, it may prove to be useful to focus on the activities of the appetite and satiety centers in the hypothalamus, once MRI techniques permit these studies.

NOTES

1. "Alzheimer's Disease," in *Kaplan and Sadock's Comprehensive Textbook of Psychiatry* (CTP), 7th ed., ed. B. J. Sadock and V. A. Sadock (Philadelphia: Lippincott Williams & Wilkins, 2000), pp. 884–85.

2. S. C. Yudofsky and R. E. Hales, *Neuropsychiatry* (Washington, DC: American Psychiatric Press, 1997), p. 262.

3. B. E. Tomlinsen, G. Blessed, and M. Roth, "Observations of Dementia in Old People," *Journal of Neuroscience* 11 (1970): 205–42.

4. In CTP, p. 170.

5. S. Salloway, P. Malloy, and J. L. Cummings, *The Neuropsychiatry of Limbic and Subcortical Disorders* (Washington, DC: APA Press, 1997), pp. 24–25.

6. J. S. Maxmen, *Essential Psychopathology* (New York: Norton, 1986).

7. Tomlinsen, Blessed, and Roth, "Observations of Dementia," pp. 205–42.

8. Reports in press for *Clinical Neuroscience Research* at the time of this writing.

9. C. van der Velde and M. W. Gordon, "Biochemical and Pharmacological Variations in Manic-Depressive Illness," *American Journal of Psychiatry* 129 (1972): 337–42.

10. G. E. Pickard and P. J. Sollars, "Biological Rhythms," in *Biological Bases of Brain Functions and Disease*, ed. A. Frazer, P. B. Molinoff, and A. Winokur (New York: Raven Press, 1994).

11. Ibid.

12. Van der Velde and Gordon, "Biochemical and Pharmacological Variations," pp. 337–42.

13. In *Biological Bases of Brain Functions and Disease*, ed. Frazer, Molinoff, and Winokur.

14. D. R. Weinberger, K. F. Berman, R. F. Zee, "Physiologic Dysfunction of Dorso-Lateral Prefrontal Cortex in Schizophrenia," *Archives of General Psychiatry* 43 (1986): 114–24.

15. A. J. Saykin et al., "Neuropsychological Function in Schizophrenia. Selective Impairment in Memory and Learning," *Archives of General Psychiatry* 48, no. 7 (1991): 618–24.

16. A. C. Lahti, H. H. Holcomb, D. R. Edoff, and C. A. Tamminga, "Ketamine Activates Psychosis and Alters Limbic Blood Flow in Schizophrenia," *NeuroReport* 6, no. 6 (1995): 869–72.

17. Carol A. Tamminga, "Neuropsychiatric Aspects of Schizophrenia," in *Neuropsychiatry of Limbic and Subcortical Disorders*, ed. S. Salloway, P. Malloy, and J. L. Cummings (Washington, DC: APA Press, 1997), pp. 855–82.

18. R. Kellner, *Psychosomatic Syndromes and Somatic Symptoms* (Washington, DC: APA Press, 1994).

19. Tamminga, "Neuropsychiatric Aspects of Schizophrenia," pp. 855–82.

20. C. van der Velde, "Variability in Schizophrenia—Reflection of a Regulatory Disease," *Archives of General Psychiatry* 33 (1976): 489–96.

21. Sigmund Freud and Joseph Breuer, "Case Study—Fraulein Anna O," in *Studies on Hysteria*, vol. 3, Pelican Freud Library (Harmondsworth: Penguin, 1974).

22. Kellner, *Psychosomatic Syndromes*.

23. M. F. Reiser, *Mind, Brain, Body* (New York: Basic Books, 1984).

21

PSYCHOTHERAPY

With a mixture of benign sarcasm and paradox, V. C. Raimy wrote in 1950, "[P]sychotherapy is an undefined technique applied to unspecified problems with unpredictable outcome. For this technique, we recommend rigorous training."[1]

Two years later, H. J. Eysenck published his review of the outcome of psychotherapy conducted with some seven thousand patients. He concluded that "this review failed to support the proposition that psychotherapy with neurotics is not more effective than no therapy at all."[2] This conclusion prompted a variety of carefully structured studies in the United States to prove the opposite. They merely showed how difficult it is to establish the efficacy of psychotherapy because of such variables as the self-limiting nature of certain mental conditions, the personalities of patients and therapists, and the uncontrollable positive and negative influences in a patient's everyday life, as discussed in detail by C. P. O'Brien and G. E. Woody.[3]

Besides the matter of effectiveness, there also is the unsettled issue of how the "talking cure" leads to improvement of an individual's mental condition and functions. One would expect to find an answer by exploring the technique(s) applied in psychotherapy, but such effort results in the experience of a déjà vu of the last two chapters: There are at least 250 different modes of psychotherapy, yet none of them are accompanied by a rationale of how they affect the mind.

Why this astonishing plethora of psychological treatment modalities? Are they all effective, and equally so? The APA Commission on Psychotherapies published in 1982 its literature review of six hundred comparative psychotherapy outcome studies. It concluded that 66 percent of all studies showed a positive effect but no evidence to suggest that any specific type of psychotherapy was more effective than any other.

Concerns among psychologists about "the proliferation of brand-name therapies leading to theoretical fragmentation and dissonant rival claims" incited their attempts to integrate the different theoretical systems and to combine the various psychotherapeutic methods into one "eclectic" system. These attempts led in 1982 to the founding of the *International Journal of Integrative and Eclectic Psychotherapy*, succeeded by the following two studies.

J. K. Zeig, founder and director of the Milton H. Erickson Foundation in Arizona, organized in 1985 a conference on the evolution of psychotherapy. Twenty-six master clinicians and theoreticians representing major contemporary disciplines were invited and asked to address the following questions: How does one define psychotherapy? What are the basic premises and underlying assumptions in their approach to facilitate change? What are the benefits and limitations of such approach?

There was no unanimity in answers to any of these questions. As Zeig summarized: "[T]here was no capsule agreement on which the speakers could agree." In 1990 Zeig and W. M. Munion expanded this study by questioning ninety-one experts of various schools of psychotherapy. Each expert was asked to provide a seventy-five-word definition of psychotherapy as he or she practiced it, a five-hundred-word qualification of the theoretical underpinnings and goals of psychotherapy, and a five-hundred-word critique of his or her approach.[4] Again, no compatible definition of psychotherapy or its process emerged, yet there was universal agreement about the importance of a positive psychotherapeutic relationship. Zeig and Munion compiled the results of this survey in their volume *What Is*

Psychotherapy? concluding that "it may be impossible to compose an encompassing definition of psychotherapy."[5]

N. Saltzman and J. C. Norcross investigated the feasibility of "integration and convergence."[6] During the years 1986 to 1989, they sent nine case studies of different diagnostic categories to thirty-four well-known psychotherapists (twenty-eight psychologists and six psychiatrists) of diverse persuasions who were assigned to panels of three or four members, each panel responding to one case study. The participants were asked to develop a diagnostic formulation, describe their desired therapeutic relationship and the patient's reaction to it, describe their treatment method, discuss the convergence and divergence of their recommendation, and describe how therapy would proceed from the first session.

The therapists were contacted again in 1990 and this time provided with copies of the original contributions by their fellow panel members. They were asked to review the accuracy and clarity of their own original descriptions, review the copies of the original formulations of their fellow panelists, and elaborate their agreements and disagreements in regard to therapeutic relationship and methodology. Agreements existed only on the formulations of patient's characteristics and the importance of the psychotherapeutic relationship, while disagreements in specificity of techniques and in patient's characteristics were considerable. The investigators concluded their volume *Therapy Wars, Contention and Convergence in Differing Clinical Approaches* by quoting Carlo Diclemente: "Psychotherapy continues to elude formal consensus and integration, while becoming more homogeneous at the level of practice."[7]

The persistent inability to define psychotherapy or to unify the different psychotherapeutic techniques into one eclectic model is generally attributed to the lack of common ground, reflecting the differences between the individual philosophies underlying the various theoretical formulations and technical models. However, this rationale overlooks the fact that all psychotherapeutic modalities were developed during the last century without the availability of a clearly defined concept of the mind, the very object of psychotherapy. Without such knowledge, not only is it extremely difficult to conceive the psychopathology of abnormal mental conditions and the nature of the psychotherapeutic process, it also confines the practice of psychotherapy to an *empirical* undertaking without the benefit of understanding how such treatment affects the mind.

When we apply the principles of the cerebral/empirical model of the mind as described below, it appears possible to arrive at a unified approach to the theory and practice of psychotherapy.

DEFINITION

Since every form of psychotherapy involves interpersonal interactions, psychotherapy can be defined as an intentionally arranged interpersonal relationship between a psychotherapist and another human being who seeks to ameliorate a psychic conflict, emotional distress, or some anomalous behavior.

This definition, which is consistent with the general spirit of the definitions proposed in the studies discussed above and in the general literature, enables us to apply the psychological and neurophysiological dynamics of human interactions, as conceived in part 4, and so identify the nature of the four essential ingredients of psychotherapy: therapeutic alliance, transference, psychotherapeutic relationship, and the psychotherapeutic process.

PSYCHOTHERAPEUTIC ALLIANCE

The traditional definition of therapeutic alliance in the *CTP–II* reads: "the collaboration between therapist and patient in which the former aims to create an alliance with the conscious adult ego of the patient and to encourage the patient to be a scientific partner in the exploration of the patient's problem."[8]

However, the control of such partnership is not exclusively in the hands of the therapist. While the patient's motivation to seek help from a professional who has made himself or herself available for that very purpose implies the mutual intention of a good working relationship, Freud observed that certain developments in the patient's notions and feelings about the therapist during the course of therapy began to interfere with the progression of the therapeutic process. This observation led to his formulation of the concept of *transference*, considered by Lewis Wolberg to be Freud's most significant discovery.[9]

TRANSFERENCE

With this concept, Freud referred to the patient's projections of feelings and fantasies attached to significant people in the patient's past onto the therapist. These fantasies were largely erotic in nature and presumed to reflect unacceptable thus repressed desires and, therefore, "transferred unconsciously."

The analysis of *positive* transference (patient's yearning for an idealized parental figure) still has an important place in contemporary psychoanalytic theories of psychotherapy. Because of its eroticized nature of the psychoanalytic notion of transference, the term is at present barely used in most nonanalytic schools of psychotherapy, as was evident from the above-mentioned studies.

However, the transference of psychological meanings of previous human relationships to future personal interactions is not isolated to erotic conditions per se, nor is it an exclusively unconscious phenomenon. As detailed in chapters 15 and 17, transference *is a natural by-product of our formations of extraneous body images.* During every human encounter, extraneous body images are automatically, instantaneously, and irresistibly activated by the appearances and actions of others, hand in hand with their mnemonically fused emotional, somatoceptive, or conceptual qualities. Thus, when meeting an unknown person, any similarity in that person's speech, gestures, or physiognomy with those of a known person will lead to the projection of one's feelings and opinions onto the person in the new relationship and thus influence our assessment of and interaction with that person accordingly. Transference is, thus, a ubiquitous, natural, and unavoidable mental phenomenon experienced by all human beings under all conditions and thus also occurs during psychotherapy in both patient and therapist, irrespective of its positive or negative subjective nature.

Consequently, while the therapist is continually alert for the appearance of physical signs of anxiety, depression, or mental "slips," he or she cannot help being also influenced by the patient's looks, demeanor, mannerisms, sincerity, spontaneity, and other personality characteristics. The patient, in turn, discerns from the therapist's tone of voice, manners, and facial expressions whether he or she is genuinely interested, compassionate, or fosters a professional aloofness. Furthermore, these observations are generally made with an acute or at least subconscious awareness.

PSYCHOTHERAPEUTIC RELATIONSHIP

The mutual, nonverbal assesments described above are the fundamental elements that create the atmosphere of the psychotherapeutic relationship between patient and therapist and, consequently, affect the psychotherapeutic alliance. The patient's attractiveness or intelligence or the nature of the symptoms or mental problem may stimulate or cool the therapist's enthusiasm in his or her therapeutic efforts. Positive feelings about the therapist may make the patient feel comfortable and secure "to open up." A negative relationship caused by a distant, uninvolved therapist may cause a patient's resistance to relate to the therapist, as might be the case when, for example, the therapist's looks or demeanor activate unpleasant memories of a strict, punitive father or domineering mother figure.

Some psychotherapeutic schools urge therapists to not engage in efforts that promote a positive psychotherapeutic relationship but to maintain a nonrapportive conduct. However, any effort by the psychotherapist to rigidly suppress behavioral, vocal, or physiognomic expressions of his or her feelings or opinions brings into the psychotherapeutic relationship an unnatural and undesired dimension that deprives patients of the benefits of experiencing the genuine and caring feelings of the therapist as a real human being. In fact, open discussions of transferred positive or negative feelings and associated mental contents toward the therapist usually contribute to a positive psychotherapeutic relationship, which was considered in all studies the most important contributing factor to psychotherapeutic alliance.

PSYCHOTHERAPEUTIC PROCESS

Psychotherapy was introduced at the end of the eighteenth century by Freud as a strictly psychological process. Since then, some 250 psychotherapeutic models have been introduced, yet the nature of their underlying process has yet to be established. Serendipitous discoveries from 1954 on also made it possible to improve mental conditions by altering cerebral conditions. Phenothiazines reduced schizophrenic symptoms; tricyclic agents lifted depressions; lithium tempered manic states; and behavior therapy proved to be effective in phobias, like biofeedback is in psychosomatic conditions.

There presently are, then, two distinctly different categories of psychotherapy: *biological* therapies, which improve mental functions by altering the intensity of cerebral activities, and the traditional *psychological* psychotherapies, which address the mind *directly* and are *contextually focused*, that is, focused on the cognitive or subjective *content* of specific mental experiences. That 66 percent of the psychological psychotherapies result in *lasting* psychological changes also suggests the involvement of a cerebral component. The identification of such a component (proposed below) would lend support to the notion that successful psychotherapy is not a placebo effect of a kind and understanding psychotherapist but explicable as a veritable cerebral procedure.

Because psychological psychotherapy is conducted by means of verbal communication in an interpersonal setting, the only possible strategy to conceive the process by which the therapist's orations convert into lasting changes in a patient's mental functions is to apply the *cerebral* dynamics of human's verbal communications, as conceived in chapter 9.

Talking and listening are the opposite products of the same neurophysiological events in the central nervous system, namely, our auditory experiences. These events are autonomously and instantaneously recorded (in the left hemisphere) as *auditory engrams,* which are *mnemonically fused* with the memories of the following three categories of experiences:

1. simultaneously formed *visual engrams* (stored in the right hemisphere), whose content (gestalts) reflects the circumstances of occurrence, locale, people's physical appearances and one's own bodily appearances, and activities;
2. memories of simultaneously experienced *emotional and somatic* sensory experiences (stored in the hippocampus and secondary sensory homunculus); and
3. *linguistic engrams* (stored in the left visual association cortex), which are the neuronal foundations of our verbal abilities.

This neural network explains how we *instantly recognize* recurring auditory experiences, how we *internally, that is, mentally, review* previous auditory experiences, and how we *verbally* describe them, including their associated *emotional and somatic* memories, by the reversed use of the neural network.

Consequently, while listening to the patient's descriptions during the earliest "psychodynamic" explorations, the therapist *inevitably* collects a large number of auditory mental representations of the patient's verbalizations, which create within the therapist's mind an "extraneous" conceptual conglomerate of the mental representations that reflect the patient's mind and that are mnemonically fused with the therapist's extraneous body images of the patient. Thus, a psychotherapist with a full-time practice amasses during his or her career hundreds of different "extraneous minds."

Once the therapist has acquired a comprehensive insight into the patient's mental assets and the origin and dynamics of pathological mental or behavioral activities and feels positive about the psychotherapeutic alliance, the therapist then faces the actual task of psychotherapy. He or she has two choices: select one of the some 250 therapeutic models advanced in the literature or apply (as many psychologists and psychiatrists are likely to do) her or his personal experience and design a treatment plan tailored to the patient's mental problem(s) and his or her uniquely personal mental capabilities. *This "freelance" approach turns out to be the only psychotherapeutic "technique" whose dynamics can be fully rationalized by virtue of the cerebral/empirical concept of the mind.*

According to this concept, the term *mind* is a verbal reference to a *conceptual entity* of innumerable mental representations (see chap. 4). Because we normally experience only one given mental representation at any time (see chap. 10), "the" mind cannot be the target of any known form of psychotherapy. Only by virtue of the retrievability of mental representations is it possible for the patient to communicate to the therapist the cognitive content of troublesome thoughts or memories and the nature of their mnemonically fused emotional or somatic qualities and so enable the therapist to decide which mental representations require adjustment. *The above implies that psychotherapy is not the treatment of the mind as the term suggests but the treatment of its constituents.*

Because of their cerebral foundation, and the fact that the autonomously operating limbic system is the provider of their psychic energy (see chap. 10), faulty or painful mental representations cannot be *mentally* eradicated. The therapist's only option to promote changes is to modulate the cognitive content or emotional meaning of a specific memory or idea by means of a joint review with the patient of "culpable" or discongruent representations. (This approach thus deviates from the Freudian psychotherapeutic objective, namely, to resolve an individual's conflicts between the hypothetical mental structures ego, superego, and id.)

Beginning with the least discomfortable mental representations, the therapist explores patient's notions of "suspected" thoughts or ideas and the appropriateness of interpretations of associated subjective aspects and offers, directly or indirectly, alternative interpretations or different modes of verbal or behavioral interactions with others. For instance, the discussion of the psychological functions of the patient's body images (which are generally overlooked in most forms of psychotherapy) enables the therapist to review with the paralyzed patient discussed in chapter 20 why and how the brain eliminated the function of a given body part—because it was associated with socially questionable implications. *Extraneous* body images also are helpful instruments in a variety of circumstances. For example, a therapist can illustrate to a paranoid patient how we normally interpret the intentions of others by judging their appearance, looks, and actions *based on our personal emotions and notions* attached to all our extraneous body images formed earlier in life, which therefore do not always provide realistic readings and anticipations of the appearances and actions of others. They are most useful during group therapy to analyze and describe the behaviors of group members and humans in general or in family therapy and marital counseling when a spouse's given style or habits are reminiscent of a disliked family member of the spouse and thus a source of irritation.

Elicitation of the *origins* (parents, siblings, teachers, coaches, and peers, as detailed in chapters 15 and 16) of the subjective qualities attached to these mental representations not only are helpful to illustrate to the patient the origins of his or her personality makeup and self-concept but also why and how the patient organizes his interactions with others. These functional discussions should also include the dialectical nature of human interpersonal relationships and interactions to emphasize that others also use their body images in uniquely personal ways.

Both forms of body images are also used in such psychological defense mechanisms as reaction formation, like the ever-smiling hostile personality. Indications of the possible existence of repressed memories or motivations may require a sodium amytal interview or a hypnotic anamnestic session in view of the biological nature of repression (see chaps. 15 and 16).

This direct and "open" approach to assess and modulate mental representations as described above is equally applicable with "intellectual" mental representations, which do not reflect material objects as a reference, like the human body, but are sheer empirical notions that are retrievable only by virtue of their mnemonic fusions with specific linguistic engrams. The assessment and discussion of these invisible, purely personal mental entities not only demand of the therapist the utmost sensitivity and mental capability to understand the patient's thoughts, which the therapist cannot see—just like he cannot feel the patient's feelings—but also the ingenuity to lucidly formulate suggestions or changes within the reach of patient's comprehensibility and interest. All this is captured in what A. Rothenberg called "the creative process of psychotherapy."[10]

As the therapist forms a conceptual conglomerate of the patient's mind, so does the patient acquire an extraneous mind of the therapist, consisting of his extraneous body images of the therapist, which are mnemonically fused with the therapist's comments and suggestions pertaining to troubling mental representations targeted by the therapist, including the positive and negative emotions experienced during all sessions. The cerebral foundation of these internalized discussions enables the patient to later mentally review treatment sessions and compare the differences between his or her own views with those of the therapist and the potential benefits of their implications. Whether the patient will implement any suggested changes depends upon the positive nature of the psychotherapeutic relationship.

Because all mental and emotional details discussed above involve cerebral and neurophysiological dynamics, they also explain the benefits of behavior therapy and hypnotic therapy.

There are at least two lines of support for the role of mental representations in psychotherapy, as conceived above. In his volume *Mental Images and Psychotherapy*, M. J. Horowitz describes how he had his patients make drawings of the content of given mental represations and how these drawings facilitate the interpretation of underlying psychopathology and the preparation of the most effective psychotherapeutic approach.[11]

The second line of support emerges when we observe the video recordings of the specific therapeutic techniques employed by the legendary psychotherapists like Frits Perls (*gestalt* therapy), Heinz Kohut (*ego* therapy), Carl Rogers (*self*-therapy), Eric Berne (*transactional* therapy), Eric Erikson (*identity* crises), and Aaron Beck (*cognitive* therapy). These therapeutic models were developed during the second half of the last century when the id, ego, and superego were the universally accepted mental structures and considered to be the source of all mental experiences and functions. The cerebral/empirical theory suggests that our sense of cognition, ego, and consciousness are the natural products of a dialectical triad (see chap. 4) and thus are integral components of all mental experiences. Because of their dialectical, that is, empirical nature, they are "untreatable." Nonetheless, all therapists proved to be extremely successful in spite of the diversity of techniques applied. However, the analysis of the video recordings of their therapy sessions shows that they all had one aspect in common, namely, every therapist invariably applied his particular technique by blending his theoretical formulations with patients' stated thoughts, concerns, behaviors, feelings, wishes, fears, and faults (all components of mental representations) and suggesting how the patient should and could act, feel, think, or avoid.

This analysis showed another common feature among all of these therapists: their emotional rapport with each of their patients, their genuine display of empathy, and their enthusiasm and patience, reflecting, perhaps, the most critical factor in successful psychotherapy: the therapist's personality and overall demeanor.

Finally, if the cerebral/empirical theory of the mind is indeed the correct answer to the psychological and psychiatric issues discussed in this volume, it then also serves as a tribute to Freud's foresight mentioned in the opening line of our introduction: "[T]here is no mind without a brain."

NOTES

1. V. C. Raimy, ed., *Training in Clinical Psychology* (New York: Prentice-Hall, 1950).

2. H. J. Eysenck, "The Effects of Psychotherapy," *Journal of Consulting Psychology* 16 (1952): 319–24.

3. C. P. O'Brien and G. E. Woody, in *Comprehensive Textbook of Psychiatry* (Baltimore: Williams & Wilkins, 1980), pp. 1568–73.

4. J. K. Zeig and W. M. Munion, *What is Psychotherapy?* (San Francisco: Jossey-Bass Publishers, 1990).

5. Ibid.

6. N. Saltzman and J. C. Norcross, eds., *Therapy Wars* (San Francisco: Jossey-Bass Publishers, 1990).

7. Ibid.

8. B. J. Sadock and V. A. Sadock, eds., *Kaplan and Sadock's Comprehensive Textbook of Psychiatry* (CTP), 7th ed. (Philadelphia: Lippincott Williams & Wilkins, 2000).

9. L. R. Wolberg, *The Technique of Psychotherapy* (New York: Grune and Stratton, 1977).

10. A. Rothenberg, *The Creative Process of Psychotherapy* (New York: W. W. Norton, 1987).

11. M. J. Horowitz, *Image Formation and Psychotherapy* (New York: Jason Aronson, 1983).

BIBLIOGRAPHY

Allport, G. W. *Pattern and Growth in Personality.* New York: Holt, Rinehart and Winston, 1961.

Arnold, M. B. *Memory and the Brain.* Hillsdale, NJ: Lawrence Erlbaum Associates, 1984.

Aronoff, J., A. I. Rabin, and R. A. Zucker. *The Emergence of Personality.* New York: Springer, 1987.

Aserinsky, E., and N. Kleitman. "Regularly Occurring Periods of Eye Motility and Concurrent Phenomena during Sleep." *Science* 118 (1953): 273–74.

Benthall, J., and T. Polhemus. *The Body as a Medium of Expression.* New York: E. P. Dutton, 1975.

Berger, M. M. *Beyond the Double Bind.* New York: Brunner/Mazel, 1978.

Blanck, R., and G. Blanck. *Beyond Ego Psychology.* New York: Columbia University Press, 1986.

Bruner, S. J. *Studies in Cognitive Growth: A Collaboration at the Center for Cognitive Studies.* New York: Wiley, 1966.

Bull, P. *Body Movement and Interpersonal Communication.* New York: John Wiley & Sons, 1983.

Bunge, M. *The Mind-Body Problem.* Oxford: Pergamon Press, 1980.

Burton, A. *Operational Theories of Personality.* New York: Wiley, 1974.

Chomsky, N., and M. Hallen. *The Sound Pattern of English.* New York: Harper & Row, 1968.

Chugani, H. T., M. E. Phelps, and J. C. Mazziotta. "Positron Emission Tomography Study of Human Brain Functional Development." *Annals of Neurology* 22, no. 4 (1987): 487–97.

Churchland, P. S. *Neurophilosophy: Toward a Unified Science of the Mind—Brain*. Cambridge, MA: MIT Press, 1986.

Cleckley, H. *The Mask of Sanity*. St. Louis: Mosby, 1964.

Critchley, M. *The Divine Banquet of the Brain*. New York: Raven Press, 1980.

Delgado, J. M. R. *Physical Control of the Mind*. New York: Harper & Row, 1969.

Denenberg, V. H., J. Garbanati, G. Sherman, D. Yutzen, and R. Kaplan. "Infantile Stimulation Induced Brain Lateralization in Rats." *Science* 201 (1978): 1150–51.

Eccles, J. C. *Brain and Conscious Experience*. Heidelberg: Springer, 1966.

———. *The Understanding of the Brain*. New York: McGraw-Hill, 1973.

Edelman, G. E. *Neural Darwinism: The Theory of Neuronal Group Selection*. New York: Basic Books, 1987.

———. *Topobiology*. New York: Basic Books, 1988.

Ekman, P., and W. V. Friesen. *Unmasking the Face*. Englewood Cliffs, NJ: Prentice-Hall, 1975.

Erikson, E. H. *Childhood and Society*. New York: Norton, 1950.

———. "Identity and the Life Cycle." *Psychological Issues* 1 (1963): 101–72.

Eysenck, H. J. "The Effects of Psychotherapy." *Journal of Consulting Psychology* 16 (1952): 319–24.

Flavell, J. H. *The Developmental Psychology of Jean Piaget*. Princeton, NJ: Van Nostrand, 1964.

Freud, S., and J. Breuer. "Case Study—Fraulein Anna O." In *Studies on Hysteria*, vol. 3. Pelican Freud Library. Harmondsworth: Penguin, 1974.

Furth, H. G. *Piaget and Knowledge*. Englewood Cliffs, NJ: Prentice-Hall, 1969.

Fuster, J. M. *The Prefrontal Cortex: Anatomy, Physiology and Neuropsychology of the Frontal Lobe*, 2nd ed. New York: Raven Press, 1989.

Gardner, H. *The Mind's New Science: A History of the Cognitive Revolution*. New York: Basic Books, 1985.

———. *Developmental Psychology: An Introduction*. Boston: Little, Brown, 1982.

Garfinkel, B. D., G. A. Carlson, and E. B. Weller. *Psychiatric Disorders in Children and Adolescents*. Philadelphia: Saunders, 1990.

Gazzaniga, M. S. *The Social Brain*. New York: Basic Books, 1987.

Geschwind, N. "Brain Disease and the Mechanisms of Mind." In *Function of the Brain*, edited by C. W. Coen. Oxford: Clarendon Press, 1985, pp. 160–80.

———. "Disconnexion Syndromes in Animals and Man." *Brain* 88 (1965): 237–94, 585–644.

Goldman-Rakic, P. "Circuitry of the Prefrontal Cortex: Short-Term Memory and the Regulation of Behavior by Representational Knowledge." In *Handbook of Physiology: Higher Functions of the Nervous System.* Bethesda, MD: American Physiological Society, 1987.

Gorman, W. *Body Image and the Image of the Brain.* St. Louis: Warren H. Green, 1969.

Gregory, R. L., and O. L. Zangwill, eds. *The Oxford Companion to the Mind.* Oxford: Oxford University Press, 1987.

Griffin, R. D. *The Questions on Animal Awareness.* Los Altos, CA: Kaufman, 1981.

Hall, C. S., and G. Lindzey. *Theories of Personality.* New York: Brunner/Mazel, 1978.

Harlow, H. F. "Social Deprivation in Monkeys." *Scientific American* 207 (1962): 136–46.

Harper, R. G., A. N. Wiends, and J. D. Matarazzo, eds. *Nonverbal Communication: The State of the Art.* New York: Wiley, 1978.

Harre, R., and R. Lamb. *The Encyclopedic Dictionary of Psychology.* Cambridge, MA: MIT Press, 1983.

Harrison, R. P. *Beyond Words.* Englewood Cliffs, NJ: Prentice-Hall, 1974.

Heath, R. G. "Electrical Self-Stimulation in Man." *American Journal of Psychiatry* 120 (1963): 571–77.

Heilman, K. M., and P. Satz. *Neuropsychology of Human Emotions.* New York: Guilford Press, 1983.

Hobson, J. A. *The Dreaming Brain.* New York: Basic Books, 1977.

Horowitz, M. J. *Image Formation and Psychotherapy.* New York: Jason Aronson, 1983.

Hubel, D. H. *Eye, Brain and Vision.* New York: Scientific American Library/Freeman, 1988.

Hunt, M. *The Universe Within.* New York: Simon & Schuster, 1982.

Isaacson, R. L. *The Limbic System.* New York: Plenum Press, 1982.

Jeannerod, M. *The Cognitive Neuroscience of Action.* Oxford: Blackwell, 1997.

Johnson-Laird, P. N. "Propositional Representations, Procedural Semantics, and Mental Models." In *Parallel Distributed Processing,* edited by D. E. Rumelhart et al. 2 vols. Cambridge, MA: MIT Press, 1988.

Jones, E. *The Life and Work of Sigmund Freud,* part 1. New York: Basic Books, 1953.

Jourard, S. *Self-Disclosure: An Experimental Analysis of the Transparent Self.* New York: Wiley Interscience, 1971.

Kandel, E. R. "Steps Toward a Molecular Grammar for Learning: Explorations into the Nature of Memory." In *Medicine, Science and Society,* edited by K. J. Isselbacher. New York: John Wiley, 1985.

—— and J. H. Schwartz, eds. *Principles of Neural Science*. New York, Elsevier, 1988.

Kaplan, H. I., and B. J. Sadock, eds. *Comprehensive Textbook of Psychiatry*. 5th ed. Baltimore: Williams & Wilkins, 1989.

Karp, D. A., and W. C. Yoels. *Symbols, Selves and Society*. New York: J. B. Lippincott, 1979.

Kaufman, D. M. *Clinical Neurology for Psychiatrists*, 3rd ed. Philadelphia: W. B. Saunders, 1990.

Kellner, R. *Psychosomatic Syndromes and Somatic Symptoms*. Washington, DC: APA Press, 1994.

Kluver, H., and P. C. Bucy. "Kluver-Bucy Syndrome." *Biological Psychiatry* 10: 65–68.

Kosslyn, S. M. "Images and Internal Representations." In *Cognition and Categorization*, edited by E. Rosch and B. B. Lloyd. Hillsdale, NJ: Lawrence Erlbaum, 1978.

Lahti, A. C., H. H. Holcomb, D. R. Edoff, and C. A. Tamminga. "Ketamine Activates Psychosis and Alters Limbic Blood Flow in Schizophrenia." *NeuroReport* 6, no. 6 (1995): 869–72.

Lauter, J., P. Herscovitch, C. Formby, and M. E. Raichle. "Tonotopic Organization in Human Auditory Cortex Revealed by Positron Emission Tomography." *Hearing Research* 20 (1985): 199–205.

Lewis, M., and F. Volkmar. *Clinical Aspects of Child and Adolescent Development*, 3rd ed. Philadelphia: Lea & Febiger, 1990.

Loftus, E. F., and G. R. Loftus. "On the Permanence of Stored Information in the Human Brain." *American Psychologist* 35, no. 5 (May 1980): 409–20.

Lorenz, K. *Studies in Animal and Human Behavior*, vol. 1. Cambridge, MA: Harvard University Press, 1971.

Lynch, G. *Synapses, Circuits, and the Beginning of Memory*. Cambridge, MA: MIT Press, 1986.

Mahler, M. S., F. Pine, and A. Bergman. *The Psychological Birth of the Human Infant*. New York: Basic Books, 1975.

Maxmen, J. S. *Essential Psychopathology*. New York: Norton, 1986.

McCarley, R. W., and J. A. Hobson. "The Neurobiological Origins of Psychoanalytic Dream Theory." *American Journal of Psychiatry* 134 (1977): 1211–21.

McCullough, W. S. "The Functional Organization of the Cerebral Cortex." *Physiological Review* 24 (1944): 390–407.

Mesulam, M. M. "Frontal Cortex and Behavior." *Annals of Neurology* 19 (1986): 320–25.

Meyer, O. G., and K. Roth. *Complex Movement Behaviors: The Motor-Action Controversy*. Amsterdam: Elsevier Science, 1988.

Mishkin, M., and T. Appenzeller. "The Anatomy of Memory." *Scientific American* (1987): 80–89.

Mountcastle, V. B. *Handbook of Physiology: The Nervous System IV*. Bethesda, MD: American Physiological Society, 1981.

Nash, J. *Developmental Psychology*. Englewood Cliffs, NJ: Prentice-Hall, 1970.

Nemiah, J. C. *Foundations of Psychopathology*. New York: J. Aronson, 1973.

Noback, C. R., N. L. Strominger, and R. J. Demarest. *The Human Nervous System*, 4th ed. Philadelphia: Lea & Febiger, 1991.

O'Brien, C. P., and G. E. Woody. In *Comprehensive Textbook of Psychiatry*. Baltimore: Williams & Wilkins, 1980, pp. 1568–73.

Pavlov, I. P. *Conditioned Reflexes*. London: Clarendon, 1927.

Penfield, W., W. Feindel, C. Hendel, and C. Symonds. *The Mystery of the Mind*. Princeton, NJ: Princeton University Press, 1975.

Penfield, W., and L. Roberts. *Speed and Brain Mechanisms*. Princeton, NJ: Princeton University Press, 1959.

Philips, J. L. *The Origin of Intellect*. San Francisco: Freeman, 1969.

Pickard, G. E., and P. J. Sollars. "Biological Rhythms." In *Biological Bases of Brain Functions and Disease*, edited by A. Frazer, P. B. Molinoff, and A. Winokur. New York: Raven Press, 1994.

Pincus, H. P., and G. J. Tucker. *Behavioral Neurology*. New York: Oxford University Press, 1985.

Pinker, S. *How the Mind Works*. New York: Norton, 1999.

———. *Visual Cognition*. Cambridge, MA: MIT Press, 1988.

Pulaski, M. A. S. *Understanding Piaget*. New York: Harper & Row, 1980.

Raimy, V. C., ed. *Training in Clinical Psychology*. New York: Prentice-Hall, 1950.

Reiser, M. F. *Memory in Mind and Brain*. New York: Basic Books, 1990.

———. *Mind, Brain, Body*. New York: Basic Books, 1984.

Restak, R. M. *The Brain*. Garden City, NY: Doubleday, 1979.

———. *The Mind*. New York: Bantam Books, 1988.

Rosenfield, I. *The Invention of Memory*. New York: Basic Books, 1988.

Rothenberg, A. *The Creative Process of Psychotherapy*. New York: W. W. Norton, 1987.

Rumelhart, D. E., J. L. McLelland et al. *Parallel Distributed Processing*. 2 vols. Cambridge, MA: MIT Press, 1988.

Sacher, E. J., L. Hellman, D. K. Fukushima, and T. F. Gallagher. "Cortisol

Production in Depressive Illness." *Archives of General Psychiatry* 23, no. 4 (1970): 289–98.

Sadock, B. J., and V. A. Sadock, eds. *Kaplan and Sadock's Comprehensive Textbook of Psychiatry* (CTP). 7th ed. Philadelphia: Lippincott Williams & Wilkins, 2000.

Salloway, S., P. Malloy, and J. L. Cummings. *The Neuropsychiatry of Limbic and Subcortical Disorders*. Washington, DC: APA Press, 1997.

Saltzman, N., and J. C. Norcross, eds. *Therapy Wars*. San Francisco: Jossey-Bass, 1990.

Saykin, A. J., R. C. Gur, R. E. Gur, P. D. Mozley, L. H. Mozley, S. M. Resnick, D. B. Kester, and P. Stafiniak. "Neuropsychological Function in Schizophrenia. Selective Impairment in Memory and Learning." *Archives of General Psychiatry* 48, no. 7 (1991): 618–24.

Schafer, R. *Aspects of Internalization*. New York: International Universities Press, 1968.

Schilder, P. *The Image and Appearance of the Human Body*. New York: International Universities Press, 1950.

Schmidt, R. F., ed. *Fundamentals of Neurophysiology*. Translated by D. Jordan and I. Jordan. New York: Springer-Verlag, 1975.

Shapiro, D. *Neurotic Styles*. New York: Basic Books, 1965.

Shepard, R. N., and L. A. Cooper. *Images and Their Transformations*. Cambridge, MA: MIT Press, 1982.

Sherrington, C. S. *Integrative Action of the Nervous System*. London: Yale University Press, 1923.

Smith, J. A., and W. D. Ross, eds. *The Works of Aristotle*. Oxford: Oxford University Press, 1910.

P. Solomon et al. *Sensory Deprivation*. Cambridge, MA: Harvard University Press, 1961.

Sperry, R. W. "Lateral Specialization in the Surgically Separated Hemisphere." In *The Neurosciences: Third Study Program*, edited by F. Schmitt and F. G. Worden. Cambridge, MA: MIT Press, 1974.

Spiegel, J. P., and P. Machotka. *Messages of the Body*. New York: Free Press, 1974.

Spitz, R. *The First Year of Life*. New York: International Universities Press, 1965.

Springer, S. P., and G. Deutsch. *Left Brain, Right Brain*, 2nd ed. San Francisco: W. H. Freeman, 1985.

Squire, L. R. *Memory and the Brain*. New York: Oxford University Press, 1987.

Stern, D. N. *The Interpersonal World of the Infant.* New York: Basic Books, 1985.

Stone, L. J., and J. Church. *Childhood and Adolescence.* New York: Random House, 1979.

Stone, L. J., H. T. Smith, and L. B. Murphy. *The Competent Infant.* New York: Basic Books, 1973.

Straus, E. W., and E. Y. H. Natanson. *Psychiatry and Philosophy.* New York: Springer-Verlag, 1969.

Tamminga, Carol A. "Neuropsychiatric Aspects of Schizophrenia." In *Neuropsychiatry of Limbic and Subcortical Disorders.* Washington, DC: APA Press, 1997, pp. 855–82.

Tinnen, L. "The Anatomy of the Ego." *Journal of Psychiatry* 52 (1989): 404–409.

Tomlinsen, B. E., G. Blessed, and M. Roth. "Observations of Dementia in Old People." *Journal of Neuroscience* 11 (1970): 205–42.

van der Velde, C., and M. W. Gordon. "Manic-Depressive Illness, Diabetes Mellitus, and Lithium Carbonate." *Archives of General Psychiatry* 21 (1969): 478–85.

———. "Biochemical and Pharmacological Variations in Manic-Depressive Illness." *American Journal of Psychiatry* 129 (1972): 337–42.

van der Velde, C. "Variability in Schizophrenia—Reflection of a Regulatory Disease." *Archives of General Psychiatry* 33 (1976): 489–96.

———. "Body Images of One's Self and of Others: Developmental and Clinical Significance." *American Journal of Psychiatry* 142, no. 5 (1985): 527–37.

Van Hoesen, G. W., B. T. Hyman, and A. R. Damasio. "Entorhinal Cortex Pathology in Alzheimer Disease." *Hippocampus* (1991): 1–8.

Von Neumann, J. *The Computer and the Brain.* New Haven, CT: Yale University Press, 1958.

Weinberger, D. R., K. F. Berman, and R. F. Zee. "Physiologic Dysfunction of Dorso-Lateral Prefrontal Cortex in Schizophrenia." *Archives of General Psychiatry* 43 (1986): 114–24.

Weinberger, D. R. "Implications of Normal Brain Development for the Pathogenesis of Schizophrenia." *Archives of General Psychiatry* 44 (1987): 660–69.

Wolberg, Lewis R. *The Technique of Psychotherapy.* New York: Grune and Stratton, 1977.

Yudofsky, S. C., and R. E. Hales. *Neuropsychiatry.* Washington, DC: American Psychiatric Press, 1997.

Zeig, J. K., and W. M. Munion. *What is Psychotherapy?* San Francisco: Jossey-Bass, 1990.

INDEX